The Challenge

Dare to Weigh the Evidence!

by

Curt Blattman

authorHOUSE®

AuthorHouse™
1663 Liberty Drive, Suite 200
Bloomington, IN 47403
www.authorhouse.com
Phone: 1-800-839-8640

Unless otherwise indicated, Scripture quotations are taken from the *New American Standard Bible,* copyright © 1960, 1962, 1963, 1968, 1971, 1972, 1973, 1975, 1977 by the Lockman Foundation. Used by permission.

Scripture quotations indentified *KJV* are from the *King James Version* of the Bible.

Scripture quotation identified *LB* is from *The Living Bible,* copyright © 1971 by Tyndale House Publishers, Wheaton, Illinois.

First published by AuthorHouse 12/10/2007

ISBN: 978-1-4343-3002-4 (sc)

Printed in the United States of America
Bloomington, Indiana

This book is printed on acid-free paper.

Dedication

This book is dedicated to the Holy Spirit, whose teaching, guidance, wisdom and love made this book possible and a sheer joy to write.

Introduction

This book is about another book, called the Bible. Now before you start asking yourself, "Why should I want to read a book that is about another?" let me ask you a question: Have you ever read the Bible?

No other book in the history of mankind has been read more than the Bible. Nor has any other book come under more debate.

Back in 1981, if someone had asked me if I had read this most remarkable book, I would have answered, "No, and why should I?" I used to think that the only reason someone would want to read the Bible was because he was looking for a crutch.

Today, if asked the same question, my answer would be: "Yes; and I have read it over and over and over again."

Why this change of attitude? Have I given in and found my crutch? Have I lost my mind? Or perhaps have I found that within its pages there is actually a message that is quite relevant for today?

The purpose of this book is to challenge your intellectual curiosity about a book that is like no other book ever written. *The Challenge* will take you on an excursion into the world of the best-selling book of all time—The Bible.

My main contention, which I plan to explore with you in *The Challenge,* is that from an intellectual, philosophical, psychological, historical, scientific, literary, logical, ethical or just about any other angle or facet, the Bible stands head and shoulders above every other book ever penned.

Because of the Bible's incredible influential nature in world history, its truly remarkable, sound intellectual scope, and its wonderful message of hope and meaning for our troubled planet, the Bible extends an open invitation to be examined by believing Christians as well as skeptics and non-believers.

As you read the following chapters, I ask only one favor: keep your mind open and be prepared to enter on a journey into a universe of extraordinary beauty, hope and meaning.

Contents

Chapter 1
You Are Extraordinary

It has been said that we are but a speck on a speck within a speck. As you read on, consider the following: You are but one of 6 billion human beings on this planet called Earth; you are a mere speck in comparison to this vast sea of humanity.

Astronomers tell us that the stars in our own Milky Way Galaxy alone number over 100 billion, and that our galaxy is one of but billions and perhaps trillions of other galaxies. Thus, our own planet Earth is but one heavenly body amidst countless trillions upon trillions of others. If one person is a speck among 6 billion, imagine how minute a speck our planet becomes among untold trillions.

But what of the concept of time? Time seems to be one dimension that has no beginning or end, but just continues on into eternity. In this dimension, the seventy to eighty years that most people can expect to live today seem nothing more than a statistical blip in time when measured against eternity.

Yes, when we view ourselves against such vast numbers, we can only stand in awe at how infinitely small a role we seem to play in the scope of our universal history.

Before you started reading this, I am sure that you thought of yourself as someone of high importance and value, not as a speck. If this were not humiliation enough, we get an even bleaker picture of who we are if we worship at the shrine of science.

Most of us have been taught at one time or another that man has evolved through an evolutionary process, that, starting with very primitive single-cell creatures, we have evolved to what we are today, over a period of a few billion years. Further, we are told that this all came about by chance from inanimate matter.

Science teaches that in essence we came about by chance. Unfortunately science has nothing to say about what happens to you after you die, except that you will soon decay and go back to nothing. If this is so, we came from nothing, and when we die we are going back to nothing. Therefore, somehow for the seventy or eighty years we are here, we must find meaning in between these two states of nothingness. If that's true, not only are you a speck, but a speck that has come about by chance.

You Are Extraordinary

Now wait a minute. The title of this chapter is "You Are Extraordinary." Certainly, from what I have presented so far, you would have every right to call into question just how extraordinary a chance speck (such as you) can really be.

Unfortunately, if one views the universe from the cold, hard, meaningless viewpoint that science offers us, there can be little hope of demonstrating this chapter title.

But there is a book that does indeed tell us just how truly extraordinary we really are. That book is the Bible.

In the next chapter, I plan to give some history and comments about this most amazing book, but right now, in order not to lose the flow of our thoughts, let's see what this book has to say about you.

In the Book of Psalms we read,

> *For Thou didst form my inward parts;*
> *Thou didst weave me in my mother's womb.*
> *I will give thanks to Thee*
> *For I am fearfully and wonderfully made...*

> Psalm 139:13-14

The Holy Scriptures clearly present us with another explanation of ourselves. In contrast to being a randomly generated speck, we are told that God Himself made us, and that we are fearfully and wonderfully made. God did such a fabulous job in creating us that when we view ourselves as God sees us we will come away with a new appreciation of just how extraordinary we really are.

Thank You, Science

Within the last 100 years, this field of study, while still holding fast to its theory of evolution, has played a large part in substantiating the biblical viewpoint of how magnificently made we are.

The Bible talks about creation, while science speaks of evolution. So much has been written on this subject that I really don't think it is profitable to go into much detail here. But I would like to make a few observations that will challenge you to the utmost of your intellectual capacity.

My main contention is that the biblical doctrine of creation should be taught alongside evolution in the school systems of today, and let the students decide which makes more sense. This sadly is not the case in almost every school in our country.

In the last 100 years there has been an explosion of scientific knowledge in the fields of human anatomy and cellular biology. Thanks to this incredible amount of factual knowledge, I feel that I can defend the following "mind-blowing" statement with no difficulty at all:

> When you were first conceived, you were the product of the fertilization process of a male sperm and a female egg cell. Biologists tell us that you today, as you are reading this book, consist of over 100 trillion cells, and that all of them came from this original single cell. But what I contend is that this one single cell, within its deep makeup, had more knowledge contained in its tiny nucleus than all the accumulated knowledge of mankind from the history of its beginning until now. Wow.

Each human cell is basically similar in composition. Each one is made up of a substance called cytoplasm. Within the core resides the nucleus, which acts as a command center. Deep inside the nucleus of every human cell we find forty-six chromosomes. Each of these contains tiny substances called genes. These genes determine your various traits, such as your hair color, your weight and the 1,001 other characteristics that make you unique.

But making up each gene we find a substance called DNA (deoxyribonucleic acid), which is the basic building block of life.

Enough of cellular biology. Clearly your DNA molecules by definition must have contained all the information needed and the ability to create who you are today. All of these tiny DNA molecules reside in that single cell, preprogrammed as it were. This one cell, somehow, knew when and how to divide to form two cells, then four and then clusters of others. It knew when to begin to form tissue and muscle fibers. It knew when to form your then tiny heart, brain and all of your organs. It knows how and when to differentiate between a liver cell and a brain cell.

It knew, that one original cell, how to exchange matter and energy in such intricate ways as to form entire systems within your then tiny frame. The digestive, circulatory, urinary and respiratory systems were completed in record time, until nine months later out you came.

This incredibly complicated, magnificently orchestrated process was again somehow preprogrammed deep within the mysterious chambers of your DNA molecules.

Around the world today, there are thousands of books written on every aspect of your complex makeup. Your eyes, ears, mouth, brain, heart, liver, hands and all the internal systems mentioned earlier have had countless thousands of technical volumes devoted to their study. Each of the above areas alone has its own doctor specialists. These wonderfully skilled and dedicated men and women have gone to medical schools for up to ten years just to understand a single tiny aspect of your incredible human anatomy.

As we begin our third millennium since the birth of Christ, there is still much knowledge that is lacking in all of the above areas. There are also so many other aspects and processes that go on within you that there is not enough space in this or any one book to mention them all.

But that one original cell knew more about these parts of your body and the processes that go on within and between them than all the textbooks ever written about them. For you see, that one cell "created them all." Its knowledge was vastly greater than all of the accumulated wisdom of science today.

You have over 100 trillion cells in all. Each cell is like a factory, pulsating with energy and performing thousands of scientifically identifiable functions within a mere millisecond, twenty-four hours a day. All 100 trillion of these vast storehouses of data are constantly interchanging matter and energy. And all are coordinated through a most amazing display of electro-chemical impulses from your brain.

Crossroads

The question must now be asked: How and where did that one single cell obtain such a seemingly limitless treasure chest of knowledge?

Science tells us that our great-great-great-etc. ancestors were the chance collision of molecules; that these molecules over vast periods of time somehow began to link themselves into primitive single-cell creatures; that they in turn, over more eons, formed more complex organisms, and on and on it went.

Could blind chance have created such incredible magnificence? Could random collisions have created genius? And could mindless matter have generated the marvelous minds we possess today?

The Bible has some other thoughts on this matter. We read in the very first chapter, in the very first verse of the Bible, the following words: "In the beginning God created the heavens and the earth" (Genesis 1:1). We read earlier (in Psalm 139:13): "For Thou didst form my inward parts; Thou didst weave me in my mother's womb." It is clearly stated in this ancient book (these words were written over 2,500 years ago) that God created the universe and He made you.

The Bible has much to say about the creative powers of God and how much He loves His creation.

It's funny how we are so quick to accept science and medicine as the definitive truth on all matters, and dismiss the Bible as a book of "old sayings" for "old people." Yet if we take any science textbook written 100 years ago, whether it be on biology, astronomy or chemistry, the best we can say is that there is much in its entertainment value but little in its scientific value. This is because, in light of present-day knowledge, a great deal of the information they contain is in error.

The Book of books, however, was written and completed almost 2,000 years ago, and has not undergone any revisions since then. I hope to explore with you, throughout the remainder of this book, how what the Bible said 2,000 years ago is completely relevant today in every aspect.

The world of science can offer us little help in discovering the deep things about ourselves. From that viewpoint we are nothing more than a chance speck in our vast and eternal universe. But as we begin to examine what God, through His vehicle the Bible, has to say, I believe you will agree that you are indeed extraordinary and here by design.

Chapter 2
Just What Is The Bible?

When O. J. Simpson was being tried for murder millions of television sets were turned on in eager anticipation of the outcome.

When Richard M. Nixon became involved in the Watergate scandal, front-page headlines were devoted to it for months. Names like Liddy and Colson became households words.

When Elizabeth Taylor and Richard Burton got divorced, the whole world wanted to know all about it.

One thing for certain can be said about these events: they generated interest and controversy whenever they were mentioned. Not only that, it seems that negative news travels fast. We love to know who, what, where and why on all subjects under the sun.

However, another interesting characteristic of ourselves is that once events seem to pass on, we lose interest in them and desire new events on which to focus.

If it's controversy that intrigues you, then may I suggest to you that the Bible, without a doubt, is the most controversial book ever written in the history of mankind.

No book has been more criticized, published, studied or smuggled into places around the world. Its message is so controversial that more people have been martyred because of their beliefs in it than for all the other books in history combined.

No book has been banned in more countries than this one book. No book has been more quoted or, for that matter misquoted than this one book. No other book has, down through the centuries, not only survived but thrived as has this one book – The Bible. In fact, one verse (John 3:16), has been translated today into approximately 2,500 different languages and dialects. This most remarkable verse reads as follows:

> *For God so loved the world, that He gave His only begotten Son, that whoever believes in Him should not perish, but have eternal life.*

Just what is the Bible? It is a book of intense controversy that has far more influence in every avenue of our lives than you might have ever imagined. Whether you have read it or not your entire life has been tremendously affected by it. As you read the following chapters, I think you will be amazed at just how profound an influence this book has had on almost every facet of your existence.

The Bible

This Bible is a collection of sixty-six different books, written by forty-plus writers over a period of 1,500 years. It is literally a big book, consisting of over 750,000 words. This is the equivalent of a 1,500-page novel.

Imagine, 1,500 years to write one book. This fact alone would easily make the Guinness Book of World Records, for the longest time ever taken to complete a book. 1,500 pages in 1,500 years comes out to one page a year or about one word a day.

This one book, however, has lasted for over 2,000 years, and today still is the best-selling book in the world. To have lasted this long, you would think that all of those forty-plus authors would have been men of high intelligence and great scholarly credentials. But the amazing thing about the Bible is that its authorship is so diverse.

Two biblical writers were kings, two were priests, two were fishermen, one was a physician, two were shepherds, one was a tax collector, one a statesman, one a soldier, one a scribe, one a theologian, and the list goes on.

Not only were these authors men of diverse occupations, but the places where they penned their contributions to this magnificent work varied significantly. One man wrote in Syria, another in Greece, one in

Italy, another in Arabia. One man wrote in a Roman prison, another in a cave (the cave of Adullam), another on a barren island (Patmos) and even one in a palace (Zion).

The contents of the Bible also show how wide and diversified its scope is: History, science, poetry, theology, ethics, philosophy, medicine, love, war and on it goes.

But throughout its entire length, the central and dominant subject is God and His relationship with man. From its very first pages right on to its final conclusion, no book is more action-packed or full of hope for mankind than this one book.

From any angle you choose to look at it, there is something most unique about this monumental book. Its themes and messages transcend time periods, transcend cultures, transcend educational backgrounds and transcend one's imagination of greatness. Is it any wonder that the first major book ever printed on Gutenberg's press was the Bible? Since 1800 over 2 billion Bibles have been printed. And no book has been translated into more languages that the Holy Bible.

It Is the Only…

If there is one book that can boast more "It is the only book" statements than the Bible, I would like to know about it.

It is the only book that gives the account of special creation (read Genesis, chapter 1)

It is the only book used to swear in people, as they take the witness stand, to tell the whole truth, in a United States court of law.

It is the only book that gives a continuous historical record from the first man to the present age.

It is the only book that boasts it will last forever; and so far, 3,000 years later, it's heading that way. For we read (in Isaiah 40:8): "The grass withers, the flower fades, but the word of our God stands forever."

It is the only book of ancient times that accurately details prophecies of events to come.

It is the only book of any religion that states man is born in sin and then presents the way of salvation.

It is the only book about which we can make the following statement: It is read by more people in the world today than any other book and banned from being read to more people on our planet than any other book.

It is the only book you will find with a whole section devoted to it in a bookstore—not a section devoted to books about the subject—The Bible—but to the Bible itself. There are so many different translations (King James Version, New American Standard, New International Version, The Amplified Bible, The Living Bible, etc.), sizes (the entire Bible, The New Testament, pocket editions, large-print editions), and materials (hardcover, paperback, leather bound) that in many of the larger bookstores an entire section is reserved for this one book.

It is the only major book that has had every word within it alphabetized. *Strong's Exhaustive Concordance of the Bible*, compiled during the last half of the nineteenth century by Dr. James Strong, professor of exegetical theology at Drew Theological Seminary, lists every word in the Bible in alphabetical order. In addition the reference and the context of every appearance of that word is given. In Dr. Strong's original work even words such as: a, an, in, I, etc., are shown, with reference to every occurrence of them. And all of this was compiled manually, without the benefit of modern computers or other electronic equipment. Can you imagine the time it must have taken to alphabetize over 750,000 words. (1)

This one very special book has quite an interesting array of credentials to recommend itself to anyone who is thinking about reading a "good book."

Indestructibility

The Bible in its own pages claims to be an eternal book. Jesus said in Matthew 24:35, "Heaven and earth will pass away, but My words shall not pass away." We read earlier (in Isaiah 40:8): "The grass withers, the flowers fades, but the word of our God stands forever." And again we read (in Psalm 119:89), "Forever, O LORD, Thy word is settled in heaven."

These are pretty strong statements to be made about a book, especially when you consider that all sixty-six books of the Bible were written between 2,000 and 3,500 years ago. In addition, there were no printing presses back then and every word had to be manually written and handed down from generation to generation on scrolls and by word of mouth.

Yet the amazing thing is that this book is still around today, despite its ancient beginnings and despite some of the most tenacious attacks ever made by mankind to see that it would never circulate again.

No book has been banned more than this one volume, from its very first printing right up until today. No book has been burned more often by its detractors than this one book. No book has been bombarded with more criticism and mocked for its content than this one book. Finally no book has been bought by more people, yet remained unopened and unread in their own homes, than the Bible.

The attempts made by people and even whole nations to destroy the Bible are so numerous, and in some cases quite hilarious, that only a few will be mentioned below.

When Nero fiddled, it is said that Rome burned. Right from the start of the completion of the Bible, sometime during the first century A.D., Christians were persecuted for their belief in this book. Nero's intense persecution of Christians around A.D. 64 was one of the earliest attempts to silence the message and the Book. However, while Rome burned, God's word continued to spread.

In A.D. 303 the Roman Emperor Diocletian tried to exterminate the Bible from Roman society by issuing a decree that every biblical manuscript be burned. But the people still held on to their precious beliefs and manuscripts, with the result that many Christians were killed and many Bibles torched. Diocletian, thinking he had accomplished what he had set out to do, erected a huge triumph column stating that this was to be a memorial proclaiming to all that the Holy Scriptures had been extinguished. However, he was a little premature since twenty-two years later a church council, meeting at Nicea, established the Bible as the only infallible judge of truth in the world. (2)

Voltaire, the great French writer and poet, back in the eighteenth century, holding a copy of the Bible in his hand, said, "In 100 years this book will be forgotten, eliminated." Funny thing, 100 years later, his house was made into the headquarters of the Geneva Bible Society. (3)

One man who had no love for this book tried to exterminate an entire race of people who cherished its Old Testament beliefs. Adolf

Hitler killed 6 million Jews during the Second World War; but the living Word of God could not be silenced.

Throughout the centuries men have used their great intellects, philosophy, hatred and even force to silence this most remarkable and resilient book. Their remains have long ago vanished and their feeble attempts to destroy this "Book of books" are now and forever recorded in the annals of history for all to see and be amused by.

Its Message

As one reads through the Bible it is hard not to come away with the idea that there is something quite different about this ancient document. Its appeal is so universal, its scope so broad and wide and its depth so incredible that it leaves any serious or even casual reader breathless.

We read (in II Timothy 3:16): "All Scripture is inspired by God and profitable for teaching, for reproof, for correction, for training in righteousness." This statement should not be taken too lightly, in view of the enormously profound effect this one book has had in molding this great country, the United States of America, into what it is today. As the next chapter will clearly show, the contents of this great book and the greatness of our magnificent country go hand in hand.

The Bible is so unique in that, although it is one book, it is not just one book. Woven into its pages we find an almost endless encyclopedia of knowledge. It is a multidimensional book that talks authoritatively on an immense array of subjects.

It is a history book. Our greatest knowledge of the ancient world comes to us through the pages of the Bible. Over the last 200 years there have been numerous archaeological discoveries in the Middle East, substantiating the accounts found in the Bible. As a result of these discoveries even the most skeptical mind must concede that the Bible is truly the history of ancient times.

It is a science book. Imagine for a moment a book 2,000 years old containing scientific statements in the fields of astronomy, chemistry and medicine that are totally accurate today. You might say, "So what is so special about that?" except for the fact our scientists didn't discover this knowledge until 1,500-plus years after the Bible said it. I can see that the skeptics are already saying that this is not possible. I will devote an entire chapter to this fascinating area, and challenge you to come to your own conclusions.

It is a book of wisdom. The Book of Proverbs, found in the Old Testament, has such an incredible wealth of wisdom on almost every avenue of human living that our lives have been guided by its principles probably without us being totally aware of it. Even the secular world acknowledges that Solomon's wisdom (he wrote most of the Book of Proverbs) is true and quite exhaustive.

But, first and foremost, running throughout its entire length, throughout its history of mankind, from Adam to Jesus, the Bible is the greatest love story ever told. No Hollywood script could ever match the Holy Scriptures and their dramatic and moving story of a God and His everlasting love for His creation.

The Plot

In the very beginning we read (in Genesis 2:7), "Then the LORD God formed man of dust from the ground, and breathed into his nostrils the breath of life; and man became a living being." The first man, Adam, God then placed in the Garden of Eden. Genesis 2:8 tells us, "And the LORD God planted a garden toward the east, in Eden; and there He placed the man whom He had formed."

From that point on the familiar story of Adam and Eve begins to unfold. Adam and Eve enjoyed wonderful fellowship with God in the Garden of Eden until one day they violated the command of God. Genesis 2:16-17 tells us about this command:

> *And The LORD God commanded the man, saying, "From any tree of the garden you may eat freely; but from the tree of the knowledge of good and evil you shall not eat, for in the day that you eat from it you shall surely die."*

When they both partook of that forbidden fruit, their fellowship with God was broken, sin entered their lives (and every single human being after them has inherited that sin nature) and the great history of humanity begins to be told.

From the fall of Adam to the close of the Holy Bible, God's great mercy, love, compassion and interaction with civilization are vividly narrated in the historical setting of the times for literally thousands of years, culminating in God's magnificent salvation plan through His son Jesus Christ.

God's dealings with mankind are depicted through the real life stories of people whose names are household words to all of us. Abraham, Moses, Samson, King David, Solomon and many others give us quite a collection of colorful history.

The lives of these people and their relationships with their God have proven so fascinating, down through the centuries, that many major motion pictures have been produced recounting the biblical narratives of their history.

Whether you believe in the reality of these accounts does not detract one bit from the enormous effect these biblical characters have had on capturing the imagination of millions through the silver screen.

The human drama is so dynamically portrayed to us that, even though it was written thousands of years ago, the stories and lives can seem totally contemporary. All of us can easily relate to so much of the human side of the Bible that it makes this book alive and fresh to each and every passing generation.

But, without a doubt, the central figure of the entire New Testament portion of the Scriptures, and for that matter the whole Bible, is Jesus Christ.

Jesus Christ

Just who was Jesus Christ? Perhaps the best way to describe who Jesus was is to list just how the Bible refers to Him throughout its pages. He has been called:

"Prince of Peace"	(Isaiah 9:6)
"The Way"	(John 14:6)
"The Lord God, The Almighty"	(Revelation 15:3)
"Savior"	(II Peter 2:20)
"The Resurrection and the Life"	(John 11:25)
"Mighty God"	(Isaiah 9:6)
"Son of God"	(John 1:34)
"The Holy One"	(Mark 1:24)
"Wonderful Counselor"	(Isaiah 9:6)

"Messiah"	(John 1:41)
"Word of Life"	(I John 1:1)
"Lord of All"	(Acts 10:36)
"Alpha and Omega"	(Revelation 1:8)
"The Cornerstone"	(Ephesians 2:20)
"Light of the World"	(John 8:12)
"King of Kings"	(Revelation 19:16)

Quite an impressive array of titles to be bestowed on any one individual, you might say. For the most widely read book in the history of our world to shower such an incredible barrage of accolades on one man should at the very least arrest our attention to ponder just what sort of a person this Jesus Christ was.

The most scholarly and influential encyclopedia in the United States, the *Encyclopedia Britannica,* clearly recognizes Jesus Christ's phenomenal impact in our world by devoting more space to this one man than to any other human being who has ever walked this earth. (4)

When we talk about impact, perhaps historian Philip Schaff summed it up best:

> "This Jesus of Nazareth without money and arms conquered more millions than Alexander, Caesar, Mohammed and Napoleon; without science or learning, He has shed more light on things human and divine than all the philosophers and scholars combine; without the eloquence of schools, He spoke such words of life as were never spoken before or since, and produced effects which lie beyond the reach of orator or poet; without writing a single line, He has set more pens in motion and furnished themes for more sermons, orations, discussions, learned volumes, works of art, and songs of praise, than the whole army of great men of ancient and modern times." (5)

The noted historian Kenneth Scott Latourette added,

"As the centuries pass, the evidence is accumulating that, measured by his effect on history, Jesus is the most influential life ever lived on this planet. That influence appears to be mounting." (6)

So, from Adam to Jesus and all in between no book has a more interesting and colorful list of personalities than the Bible. The entire New Testament is filled with the accounts of what Jesus did on earth: His teachings, miracles, love for man and His death. It is truly a monumental document of God's love for us.

Bad Press

In today's fast-paced, sophisticated and high-tech society we are constantly looking for new and better ways to do things. Old concepts and values are in a perpetual state of transformation. In order to make it today, you have to keep up with this constant state of change or else find yourself quickly being called old-fashioned.

Science is fast becoming the new altar at which we worship. We have literally placed our trust in and staked our lives on the belief that whatever problems we face in the future, our scientists will be able to answer for us.

Is it any wonder that the Bible has found little place in people's hearts and minds today? To a great majority of us, when you say the word "Bible," little enthusiasm is generated. Comments such as the following are heard: "It's an old stodgy book that may have been OK back then, when it was written; but it is outdated and hasn't kept pace with the times. Only religious people read the Bible. It's a good book but not for my generation. It's so dull."

Most of the people who make these statements have probably never read the Bible. However, they are experts on why we shouldn't read it. This bad press is quite unfortunate because it has caused many people to get a wrong impression about the Bible.

Far from being an old, stodgy, out-of-date, dull book, the Word of God is alive with action and adventure, full of incredible mysteries, quite timely for our space-age society, and full of wisdom, love and hope.

May I challenge you to judge for yourself just what type of book the Bible really is? As we travel through the remainder of this book, hold onto your hats and be prepared to journey into the pages of a book like no other book you have ever read before.

Chapter 3
God Bless America

And indeed He Has. There can be little doubt that, in all of history, no nation has experienced more continuous prosperity throughout its entire lifetime than the United States of America. You may be saying to yourself, "Yes, I know this is true," but have you ever wondered why our nation has been the recipient of such great blessings?

The answer to this question, I firmly believe, can be found in the words of one of our most patriotic hymns, "America the Beautiful":

> O Beautiful for spacious skies,
> For amber waves of grain,
> For purple mountain majesties
> Above the fruited plain!
> America! America!
> God shed His grace on thee,
> And crown thy good with brotherhood
> From sea to shining sea! (7)

God shed His grace on thee. Could this really be the cause of the greatness of our country? As with anything in life, whenever we view the outward effect of a situation, we know that somewhere there must be a cause or a reason behind the reality we see.

As we journey back through time, we cannot help but be impressed by the tremendous effect the Bible has had in molding, shaping and influencing this great nation we live in. I dare say that the Bible is as American as baseball, apple pie and Coca Cola. No book in our history has left such an indelible imprint on our very fabric and heritage as the Holy Scriptures.

Now, before you think I am being sacrilegious by placing the Bible on the same plane with such Americana as baseball and apple pie, let's examine the evidence.

The Cornerstone

Symbols play an important role in all societies around our globe. If you have ever been to New York City, one thing you will never forget is the tremendous number of skyscrapers that engulf the island of Manhattan. Many of these buildings are fifty, sixty and even 100 stories high. They stand as a shining testimony of the great heights to which our country has been able to soar during its 200-year history.

But with any great structure, whether it be a building such as the Empire State Building or a country such as the United States, the key to its success lies in its strong foundation. Without a strong foundation, even great structures begin to totter, fail and fall.

To build a 100-story building we must lay a foundation deep underground before we can even start to build. And for a country such as America to have become such a magnificently prosperous and free land, it too must have been build on solid bedrock, and that bedrock was the Bible.

A Declaration of Independence

On July 4, 1776, a nation was born, and the Declaration of Independence has become our most time-honored document. However, perhaps a better name for this historic writing should have been the "Declaration of Dependence." If we read the closing words of the Declaration of Independence, we find the following: "…with a firm reliance on the Protection of Divine Providence, we mutually pledge to each other our Lives, our Fortunes, and our sacred Honor." A declaration was thus made of dependence on Almighty God.

In the book *The Rebirth of America,* reference is made to those fifty-six men who penned their names to this wonderful document:

> "The fifty-six courageous men who signed that document understood that this was not just high-sounding rhetoric. They knew that if they succeded,

the best they could expect would be years of hardship in a struggling new nation. If they lost they would face a hangman's noose as traitors.

"Of the fifty-six, few were long to survive. Five were captured by the British and tortured before they died. Twelve had their homes, from Rhode Island to Charleston, sacked, looted, occupied by the enemy or burned. Two lost their sons in the army. One had two sons captured. Nine of the fifty-six died in the war, from its hardships or from its bullets.

"Whatever ideas you have of the men who met that hot summer in Philadelphia, it is important that we remember certain facts about the men who made this pledge: They were not poor men or wild-eyed pirates. They were men of means—rich men, most of them, who enjoyed much ease and luxury in their personal lives. Not hungry men, but prosperous men, wealthy landowners, substantially secure in their prosperity, and respected in their communities.

"But they consider liberty much more important than the security they enjoyed, and they pledged their lives, their fortunes, and their sacred honor. They fulfilled their pledge. They paid the price. And freedom was won." (8)

These fifty-six men not only knew the importance of the protection of divine Providence, but also knew what kind of rights their God of the Bible guaranteed them; for we read in the second paragraph of their "Declaration":

"We hold these truths to be self-evident, that all men are created equal, that they are endowed by their Creator with certain unalienable Rights, that among these are Life, Liberty and the pursuit of Happiness…"

One of the original signers of this historic document, Thomas Jefferson (the Third President of the United States), captured the consensus of all the other signers best when he asked: "Can the liberties of a nation be secure, when we have removed the conviction that these liberties are the gift of God?"

There can be little doubt that our country came into existence through the courage and convictions of men who based their ideas and ideals on the Word of God—The Bible.

A Bell Sounds

No trip to the city of brotherly love, Philadelphia, can be called complete without stopping by to admire one of the most honored symbols of freedom in our land, the Liberty Bell. Since it came to our country from England, where it was cast in 1752, it has been an object of great reverence to Americans because of its association with our early fight for freedom from British rule.

As the Bible was the invisible hand behind the drafting of our Declaration of Independence, so too it should be impossible to separate this "Bell of Freedom" from the inscription it bore: "Proclaim liberty throughout all the land unto all the inhabitants thereof." What fitting words to describe the function of this great bell. As you might have expected, the source for these thrilling and inspiring words is from the Bible: Leviticus 25:10 (KJV).

The United States Constitution

This one document commands the respect and admiration of our entire free world. Its brilliance as a governing tool is truly extraordinary. Can anyone dispute that the greatness of our land is due to the system of government our Constitution established.

The words of its preamble still send chills through the hearts of millions who owe our founding fathers so much:

> "We, the people of the United States, in order to form a more perfect Union, establish justice, insure domestic tranquility, provide for the common defence, promote the general welfare, and secure the blessings of liberty to ourselves and our posterity, do ordain and establish this Constitution for the United States of America.."

Again, a little history of some of the thoughts that went through the minds of the men who drafted this document can provide us some insight into how important the Bible was in the conception of the Constitution.

We turn once more to *The Rebirth of America* to capture a most telling incident:

> "In the summer of 1787 representatives met in Philadelphia to write the Constitution of the United States. After they had struggled for Several weeks and had made little or no progress, eighty-one-year-old Benjamin Franklin rose and addressed the troubled and disagreeing convention that was about to adjourn in confusion.

> " 'In the beginning of the contest with Britain, when we were sensible of danger, we had daily prayers in this room for Divine protection. Our prayers, Sir, were heard and they were graciously answered. All of us who were engaged in the struggle must have observed frequent instances of a super-intending Providence in our favor ... Have we now forgotten this powerful Friend? Or do we imagine we no longer need His assistance?

> "I have lived, Sir, a long time, and the longer I live, the more convincing proofs I see of this truth: that God governs in the affairs of man. And if a sparrow cannot fall to the ground without His notice, is it probable that an empire can rise without His aid? We have been assured, Sir, in the Sacred Writings that except the Lord build the house, they labor in vain that build it. I firmly believe this...

> "I therefore beg leave to move that, henceforth, prayers imploring the assistance of Heaven and its blessing on our deliberation be held in this assembly every morning." (9)

Once more we see how the Sacred Writings, the Bible, played an important role in influencing the minds of the men who were to establish the greatest nation in the world.

The history of the beginnings of our great country is so fundamentally tied to the Bible that it is almost as if the two have become one. History itself leaves us with no doubt that the Bible was a key element molding our nation into the great country it was destined to become.

In God We Trust

Most Americans are probably unaware that they are almost constantly carrying this phrase with them, wherever they go throughout the day. In 1864 our government leaders acknowledged the important role God played in making our nation great by placing the phrase "LIBERTY – IN GOD WE TRUST" on every coin minted.

It was as if they were paying tribute to God for the blessings He had already bestowed upon them, as well as showing confidence that He would continue to bless them in the future. The next time you put your hand in your pocket or pocketbook, pull out a coin, any coin, and see how each one you choose proudly displays such an important part of our American heritage.

Listen to Your Leaders

But the Bible didn't have just Benjamin Franklin's endorsement as a valuable aide to governing a nation. Men such as John Quincy Adams, Andrew Jackson, Abraham Lincoln, Theodore Roosevelt, Woodrow Wilson and Calvin Coolidge also recognized its influence, wisdom and need to be read, not just by the elite, but by all the people of our land.

For one book to have the sixth, seventh, sixteenth, twenty-sixth, twenty-eight, and thirtieth Presidents of the United States of America strongly recommend it is quite an endorsement indeed. If the Bible were to have a book jacket and the following six presidential quotes listed, I dare say the Bible just might have made the Book-of-the-Month choice selection:

> "The first and almost the only Book deserving of universal attention is the Bible." (10) And, "The earlier my children begin to read the Bible the more confident

will be my hope they will prove useful citizens of their country and respectable members of our society."
John Quincy Adams

"Go to the Scriptures...the joyful promises it contains will be a balsam to all your troubles." (11)
Andrew Jackson

"All the good from the Savior of the world is communicated through this Book; but for the Book we could not know right from wrong. All the things desirable to man are contained in it." (12)
Abraham Lincoln

"A thorough knowledge of the Bible is worth more than a college education." (13)
Theodore Roosevelt

"...The Bible...is the one supreme source of revelation of the meaning of life, the nature of God and spiritual nature and need of men. It is the Only guide of life which really leads the spirit in the way of peace and salvation." (14)
Woodrow Wilson

"The foundations of our society and our government rest so much on the teachings of the Bible that it would be difficult to support them if faith in these teachings would cease to be practically universal in our country." (15)
Calvin Coolidge

Another President by the name of Ronald Reagan, recognized the incredible knowledge, wisdom and value of this one book by paying it tribute: declaring the year 1983 "The Year of the Bible."

Education And The Bible

In a land where so much emphasis is placed on status symbols, it is not surprising that when you mention that you are a Harvard, Yale or Princeton graduate, you command an immediate air of respect. But what is surprising is that when you look at the origins of these three schools, you find that the Bible was their cornerstone.

Back in 1636, Harvard was founded. Part of the "Rules and Precepts" adopted in 1646 contained the following:

> "Every one shall consider the main end of his life and studies to know God and Jesus Christ which is eternal life.
>
> "Seeing the Lord giveth wisdom, every one shall seriously by prayer in secret seek wisdom of Him.
>
> "Every one shall so exercise himself in reading the Scriptures twice a day that they be ready to give an account of their proficiency therein, both in theoretical observations of languages and logic and in practical and spiritual truths..." (16)

Likewise, Princeton and Yale were founded on the belief that the Bible was the key to higher education and that without its study a student would in no way be equipped to face the challenges ahead of him. Down through the decades (Princeton and Yale were founded in 1746 and 1701 respectively), the Bible became less and less a foundation in the curriculum of these schools. However, the great influence Ivy League graduates of these schools had in molding our nation in its early beginnings and throughout the 1800's is undeniably part of their great legacy to us today.

As pervasive as the Holy Scriptures were in educating those who attended our great universities, its influence on American children was equally profound. While it is true that many children during the 1700's and 1800's never really received a formal education, learning to read was considered a proud privilege. And one of the key reasons why parents wanted their children to learn to read was so that they could read the Bible.

In both higher and lower education, the Bible stood alone as both a cornerstone and status symbol. It also proved to be a great comforter in the harsh realities of life in colonial as well as post-revolutionary society. For you see, the story of America is to a large extent the story of the Word of God. Minds trained in the Scriptures were minds destined to propel our country on to greatness.

The Lost Book

Mention the Word "Bible" today and be assured that many people will have little interest in it. Not only will they have little interest in it, but you probably will make many of them uncomfortable. And on top of that, tell them that you read it, and notice that you begin to get strange looks.

While it is sad how the most revered and treasured book of our forefathers, our prestigious universities and our great beginnings has fallen into such disuse, we still can see vestiges of its influence rippling throughout the fabric of our land.

Our lower-level schools still talk about God every day when they recite the Pledge of Allegiance to the Flag:

> "I pledge allegiance to the flag of the United States of America and to the Republic for which it stands, one Nation under God, indivisible, with liberty and justice for all."

We sing our National Anthem – "The Star-Spangled Banner" – at every baseball, football, basketball and hockey game. Few people, however, know the words of the fourth stanza:

> Oh. Thus be it ever when free men shall stand
> Between their loved home
> and the war's desolation,
> Blest with vict'ry and peace,
> may the Heav'n-rescued land
> Praise the Pow'r that had made

27

and preserved us a nation.
Then conquer we must, when our cause it is just,
And this be our motto, "In God is our trust."
And the star-spangled banner
In triumph shall wave
O'er the land of the free
And the home of the brave. (17)

It is interesting to note how one part of our government, the United States Supreme Court, has ruled prayer in our schools unconstitutional, while another part, the United States Senate and House of Representatives, begin every session with prayer.

While Washington, D.C., has basically legislated God out of the schools, her very own buildings and monuments are so full of references to God and verses from the Bible that you have to wonder what is going on.

As an example consider the following:

- Engraved on the metal cap at the top of the Washington monument are the words: "Praise be to God."
- On the walls of the Library of Congress can be found many Bible verses; one such says: "The heavens declare the glory of God, and the firmament showeth His handiwork." Psalm 19:1 (KJV)
- Right above the head of the Chief Justice of the United States Supreme Court are the Ten Commandments, protected by the American eagle.

The great walls of our most influential as well as revered buildings in our capital city are like great canvases where a vast collection of scriptural quotations are displayed.

In most American homes, God's Holy Word remains wholly unopened. It may maintain a place in your bookcase or on your mantle, but not in your heart, mind or thoughts. As such, it remains a treasure house of knowledge and wisdom untapped, a great journey into the fabulous history of our ancient world unexplored, and perhaps the key reason why we enjoy such great freedom today, unrealized. My friends, this book may just be the best-kept secret in our country.

The Lesson Of History

When I went to high school, it was mandatory to study history for one period a day for all four years. To spend such a large portion of our education time on learning about things in the past tells you just how important our society thinks the study of history is. All of us are familiar with the great emphasis placed on learning about our own American history, and rightly so. The Revolutionary War, the Civil War, World Wars I and II, the industrial revolution, the thirteen original colonies, the Gold Rush, the Pony Express and many more topics are all part of our glorious past. They, in a sense, have helped mold you and me into who we are today.

The struggles to obtain and then maintain our freedoms are one continuous thread that we all can see running through our entire history. We have come to cherish the hard-fought battles previous generations have won for us. As a result of these victories, freedom rings true in all our land. Our schools fortunately realize how important it is to study about them in order to learn their causes. For to know the causes that helped to secure our liberty may just give us the clues we need to pass these freedoms down to our children and their children.

John Quincy Adams challenged us to learn from the past why America and "liberty" became two sides of the same coin to all the world around it. The sixth President of the United States once remarked,

> "Posterity, you will never know how much it has cost
> my generation to preserve your freedom. I hope you
> will make good use of it." (18)

This is the same man we quoted earlier as saying, "The first and almost the only Book deserving of universal attention is the Bible."

May I challenge you to explore some of the evidence this chapter has presented concerning the unique role the Bible has played in the shaping of this great land we live in? For if we can establish a cause-and-effect relationship between the Holy Scriptures and the great liberty we experience today, then to discard the Bible and its teachings may just mean that one day these precious freedoms will no longer be ours.

Throughout world history, down through the centuries, nations have become great and powerful and, with time, have collapsed. Empires have been built and later have come crashing down. Even dynasties have lasted for hundreds of years only to eventually dissolve. Correspondingly, the ideologies that have allowed this great rise to power have also come and gone with the decline of these countries.

The Bible, however, like a shining beacon in the night, has weathered any and every storm it has had to face over the past 3,000 years. One thing we hear over and over again is that history always repeats itself. If this is any indication, then we can be sure that nations will continue to rise and fall and that the Bible will always be there.

The American ideology and the democratic free state it has so wonderfully fostered were conceived of by men with vision, who for the most part were men guided by the tenets of the Bible. Without the Bible, the great American dream would never have become a reality.

Just as the early sailors guided themselves through the seas by using the stars as their compass, our first American ancestors anchored themselves to the Holy Scriptures as their constant companion through all the trials and battles they faced.

What has made us such a great nation? Our wonderful beginning. And what brought about that beginning? The Bible.

Chapter 4
Science–The Catch-Up Game

Aldous Huxley said, "Modern science makes it impossible to believe in a personal God." In our technological, space-age society, many scientists believe that the Bible may be an inspirational book, but that it is full of errors when it speaks on scientific matters. Evolutionists, anthropologists and the entire field of science today strongly contend that they have finally been able to disprove much of the Bible.

May the words of the Psalmist present the challenge to the above contingent of our most prestigious scientific minds who hold this belief today. We read in Psalm 19:7-9

The law of the LORD is perfect, restoring the soul;
The testimony of the LORD is sure, making wise the simple.
The precepts of the LORD are right, rejoicing the heart;
The commandment of the LORD is pure, enlightening the eyes.
The fear of the LORD is clean, enduring forever;
The judgments of the LORD are true; they are righteous altogether.

God's Word says that it is perfect, sure, right, pure, clean and true. We further read (in John 17:17): "...Thy word is truth." God Himself, the Creator of the entire universe, is telling our modern men of science that His Word has no errors, including scientific ones. This is an amazing statement, but remember that the Bible is an amazing book. The stage is set. Let's examine this most provocative area.

Science And Error

Any student of the history of science has to be impressed with the fact that this branch of knowledge has been incredibly wrong so often that one has to wonder if it really is science.

Down through the centuries so much of the discoveries of science have proven totally wrong, and many of its time-honored theories have been completely abandoned. Even hard facts (at least to their contemporaries) have been shown to be nothing more than hard fiction.

We treat our great scientists and men of medicine as if they were gods who have all the answers to life's deep mysteries and problems. The reality of the situation is, however, that if we were to keep a scorecard over the past two millennia their marks would not pass the test of time.

Many of our greatest scientists have had the discoveries that made them famous proven totally wrong. Many others who proposed ideas and theories that would later change and revolutionize our world were, at the time they proposed them, thought of as crazy, foolish and plain dead wrong. Strange how a field that prides itself on accuracy and wisdom can be in such a state of mass confusion and error.

As an example of what I am talking about, consider the following four true stories:

Svante Arrhenius

The great Swedish chemist Svante Arrhenius (1859-1927) back in 1884 came up with a theory that turned out to be a revolutionary concept for its time. His theory of ionic dissociation helped to explain why a solution of sodium chloride (table salt) could transmit electric current.

His theory stated that sodium chloride broke up into two particles, a sodium and a chlorine, as soon as it was placed in solution. Since the solution didn't contain metallic sodium and gaseous chlorine, Arrhenius reasoned that the sodium and chlorine must carry electric charges that allowed the electric current to flow through the solution.

His concept was not well received by his peers. In fact when Arrhenius presented his ionic dissociation ideas as part of his Ph.D. thesis, he was given the lowest possible passing grade.

However, only nineteen years later, in 1903, for the same thesis, he won the Nobel Prize in Chemistry. Quite a turn of events in such a short period of time.

Nicolaus Copernicus

Any schoolboy knows that the Earth revolves around the sun. Any learned man of science back in the 1400's knew something quite different. Back then they all believed that the Earth was the center of the universe and that the sun moved around the Earth. In fact, if you disagreed with this scientific "fact" you ran the risk of being branded a heretic.

Nicolaus Copernicus (1473-1543), a Polish astronomer, had a different idea. He believed that the sun, rather than the Earth, was the center of the universe. He stated that the earth and all the other planets moved through space and revolved around the sun. Copernicus was quite scared to publish this theory for fear he might be considered a heretic. Strange how his theory, back then, could have cost him his life, while the prevailing theory of his time would, if you held it today, brand you as a candidate for the "loony bin."

Ignaz Semmelweiss

Another scientist that few of you may ever have heard about was the Hungarian physician Ignaz Semmelweiss (1818-1865). The Bible says (in Proverbs 16:18), "Pride goes before destruction, and a haughty spirit before stumbling." The truth of this statement is vividly shown in the following real-life historical tragedy.

Semmelweiss was quite interested in a very puzzling disease call childbed fever. In his research, Semmelweiss observed that many women bearing children in the hospitals of Vienna, where the best-educated doctors could be found, died of very high fevers shortly after giving birth. He also observed that women bearing children at home, with the help of uneducated midwives, rarely died.

He determined that the doctors were the ones responsible for spreading the disease. It was common practice back then for a doctor to be working in the dissecting room and immediately afterward, move to the delivery room without carefully cleaning his hands. Semmelweiss, in 1847, began forcing the doctors under his charge to wash their hands in strong chemicals before touching any patients.

Many of these highly qualified doctors flatly refused to wash their hands and resented being thought the cause of spreading this disease. It became a question of pride. When the doctors washed their hands, the childbed fever rate went down. When they didn't, needless lives were lost. This was truly a black day for modern medicine.

The Germ Theory of Disease

Finally, consider what many have termed the single most important medical discovery of all time: "The germ theory of disease." Back in the fifth century B.C., Hippocrates offered his explanation of infectious disease and epidemics. He believed that epidemics were due to unfortunate weather conditions. He reasoned that the air could turn bad and that, since many people would breathe the same air, they would get sick. Since then others have believed that the air arising from swamps or refuse heaps could also contribute to the spread of disease.

It was not until over 2,000 years later that men such as Louis Pasteur, a French chemist (1822-1895), and Robert Koch, a German bacteriologist (1843-1910), determined that very tiny organisms called germs were what caused diseases. It took scientists 2,000 years to fully disregard their old ways.

The Strange Faces Of Truth

Down through the centuries, science and "the truth" have been strange bedfellows. Arrhenius and his theory of ionic dissociation is an example of the "truth confused." His contemporaries were confused as to why certain solutions could conduct an electric current.

Semmelweiss and his research on childbed fever are a classic case of the "truth hidden." The doctors in Vienna clearly knew they were wrong, but their pride caused them to hide and suppress the truth.

Copernicus claimed to the world that we were no longer the center of the universe. In his case we see a perfect example of the "truth denied." People back then flatly denied such an outrageous thought— that the Earth just might not be the center of everything.

Finally, when Pasteur and Koch discovered the germ theory of disease, they showed the world that the field of science often is in a state of the "truth unrecognized." It took over 2,000 years for the truth to become known.

Confused, hidden, denied and unrecognized. These are hardly words that describe what would come to mind if someone asked you what you thought of when you heard the word "science."

From what I have said so far you might have the impression that I am down on science and technology. This, however, is far from the case; on the contrary, I have quite a high regard for our great men of science. In fact, these great minds have done a tremendous job in improving the world we live in today, in prolonging and saving many lives and in allowing many of our dreams of yesterday to become reality today. In addition, the many scientific breakthroughs during the past 500 years have helped to demonstrate that the Bible is a most amazing science book.

The Bible And Science

Over the past thirty centuries, the Bible has been attacked as being a book full of scientific errors. While many have argued that its message is spiritual and inspiring, it unfortunately doesn't use scientific jargon and has just not been able to keep pace with the explosion of scientific knowledge.

Critics of the Holy Scriptures would certainly have a case to question the entire Bible if they could clearly demonstrate gross errors in the realm of science. The more kindhearted detractors say that when the Bible speaks on scientific matters, we should consider it in allegorical and spiritual terms since it contains so many errors.

For a God to have had the knowledge and the power to have created the entire heavens and the earth, as we read earlier in Genesis 1:1, but to lag behind the times on scientific concerns, would certainly cause one to wonder just what kind of a book the Bible really is. Fortunately, when people begin to explore the pages of the Holy Scriptures, they soon realize that they have found a vast treasure chest full of incredibly accurate data in the fields of biology, astronomy, medicine, physics, psychology and just about every branch of modern science.

Far from lagging behind the times, the Bible, when it was written, was 2,000 to 3,000 years ahead of science. What our modern men of science have been able to do is to finally validate much of what the Bible said way back when it was written. May the following six examples serve to show the open-minded that our ancient Bible is in reality modern science.

Stars In The Night

Just how many stars are there in our universe? If we were to assemble a panel of distinguished internationally known astronomers from history we would get a very interesting result.

Hipparchus, a great Greek astronomer (146-126 B.C.), estimated that there were 1,022 stars. Ptolemy, another famous Greek astronomer (A.D. 127-51), placed the number at 1,056. Tycho Brahe, a great Danish astronomer (1546-1601), calculated that there were 777 stars. Finally, the brilliant German astronomer Johann Kepler (1571-1630) cataloged 1,005.

From 100 B.C. up until the 1600's the consensus was that there were approximately 1,000 stars in the universe. Since then this estimate has been greatly increased. It is now common knowledge that our own Milky Way Galaxy contains over 100 billion stars. Most modern astronomers believe that there are also billions of galaxies just like our own. If we were to estimate 100 billion galaxies each containing 100 billion stars, we would have 10,000,000,000,000,000,000,000 stars. Clearly it is not humanly possible to count this many stars.

However, over 2,500 years ago, God spoke to the prophet Jeremiah and said (in Jeremiah 33:22), "As the host of heaven cannot be counted, and the sand of the sea cannot be measured so I will multiply the descendants of David My servant..." The Bible said 2,500 years ago that there is no way to number the stars because the universe is too vast. Only with the advent of the telescope in the seventeenth century, 2,000 years after Jeremiah, did our modern astronomers begin to catch on that the heavens had quite a bit more than 1,000 stars.

The Little Appendix

If you were to have an attack of appendicitis back in 1850, there would have been a good chance you would have died if your appendix burst. Many medical doctors during the twentieth century have argued, "If there is a God, why did He allow such a useless and functionless organ as the appendix to exist in man." In fact, up until recently, many doctors who were performing surgery on their patients on a part of the body near the appendix would snip the appendix out also (even if it was in perfect condition) as a bonus, thinking it served no function (and might cause trouble), so why keep it?

Evolutionists use to say that the appendix is just a leftover part of the body that has come about though the natural evolutionary process.

During the last thirty years, an entire new field of medicine call immunology has exploded on the scene. Many experts believe that this one field may give us the best answers and cures for our modern curse called cancer. Basically, immunology utilizes substances that are naturally found in our own bodies to help combat disease. Through intensive research, it has now become well known that a person's tonsils and appendix form an important part of our natural disease-combating defense system. Far from being useless, they help keep us ready for battle against sickness and disease.

When God created us, He knew what He was doing. There is nothing useless in our marvelous bodies, as modern medicine has finally begun to understand.

The Essence Of Life

Our internal makeup is unbelievably complex. In order to perform the thousands of different processes that are going on inside the trillions of cells within our bodies, we need to supply each one of these cells with oxygen, water and food. This is accomplished through the blood, which circulates throughout our entire body constantly from moment to moment, from year to year. The blood is also essential in combating disease. In fact the "gift of Life" is many times the gift of blood through transfusions.

This medical fact was firmly established in 1628 by William Harvey, through his observations of the circulatory system. Before that time, doctors took blood out of people in the hope of healing them. Today, we give blood to patients to speed healing. Our blood is the very network of life within us.

The Bible, far from being just a spiritual book, happens to know quite a bit of biology also. Perhaps William Harvey compared notes with the Bible, for Leviticus 17:11 says, "For the life of the flesh is in the blood." Two thousand years before William Harvey discovered one of the great keys to human life, God revealed it to us in such precise words.

It's All In Your Head

So many things today that are common knowledge were not understood even 100 years ago. One such area that has gone through two separate revolutions in thinking in this short time span is the relationship between health and sickness.

Up until the middle of the nineteenth century, bad air was thought to be a main cause of sickness and infectious disease, as we spoke about earlier. With the formulation of the germ theory of disease, bacteria was found to be the chief culprit causing many of our illnesses. During the last fifty years, our modern men of medicine have now been telling us that mental stress and our emotions are the major cause of disease ranging from ulcers to fatal heart attacks.

Psychosomatic illness is not just a "buzz word." It is a hard reality. Many doctors estimate from 50% to 80% of all our sickness and disease today find their cause in our faulty way of thinking. The intense stress and emotional turmoil we place ourselves under by our modern fast-paced lifestyle are literally deteriorating every organ in our bodies.

How this can happen can be seen if we understand that the emotional center of the brain is constantly transmitting impulses through nerve fibers to every organ and area of the body. It is now well known and medically proven that emotional stress can produce almost any illness imaginable.

The three main ways in which the emotional center produces disease and illness are by changing the amount of blood flowing to an organ, by influencing the secretions of certain glands and by affecting the tension in our muscles.

The next time you are embarrassed, notice how the blood vessels in your face open up, causing you to blush. The next time you are really scared, notice how your heart begins to beat extremely fast as your adrenal glands begin to increase their secretions. Finally, become very angry, and watch how you clench your jaw and send pain throughout your body. If we amplify these occurrences many times over many years, we can start to understand how constant emotional stress will slowly break down our entire body, weaken our disease-fighting resistance and destroy our lives.

The following chart will further illustrate this point:

EMOTIONS	DISEASE
Envy	Heart Trouble
Guilt	Diabetes

Anger	Colitis
Worry	Ulcers
Jealousy	Cancer
Hate	Constipation/Diarrhea
Fear	High Blood Pressure

You can probably draw arrows from any emotion to any disease and vice versa and over a period of twenty, thirty or forty years find a cause-and-effect relationship. 100 years ago medicine understood very little about how the mind could affect our health. Today it is a fact that stress is our number-one killer.

In the Book of Proverbs, God has so overwhelmingly shown us how the mind affects our health that it is amazing it took medical science over 2,000 years to acknowledge what the Bible has stated all along.

May the five verses below, from the Book of Proverbs, serve to demonstrate that God is indeed the "Great Physician," and that His knowledge of our emotions is right in stride with our most up-to-date findings in the field:

> *A joyful heart is good medicine, But a broken spirit dries up the bones.*
> Proverbs 17:22

> *Pleasant words are a honeycomb, Sweet to the soul and healing to the bones.*
> Proverbs 16:24

> *Anxiety in the heart of a man weights it down, But a good word makes it glad.*
> Proverbs 12:25

> *A soothing tongue is a tree of life, But perversion in it crushes the spirit.*
> Proverbs 15:4

> *A tranquil heart is life to the body, But passion is rottenness to the bones.*
> Proverbs 14:30

One hundred years ago medical science knew very little about how our emotions could influence our well being, but 2,500 years ago a man named Solomon knew all about it.

We read further, from the Book of Philippians, the best medical advice ever given out:

> *Be anxious for nothing, but in everything by prayer and supplication with thanksgiving let your requests be made known to God. And the peace of God, which surpasses all comprehension, shall guard your hearts and your minds in Christ Jesus. Finally, brethren, whatever is true, whatever is honorable, whatever is right, whatever is pure, whatever is lovely, whatever is of good repute, if there is any excellence and if anything worthy of praise, let your mind dwell on these things.*
>
> Philippians 4:6-8

Perfect Order

One of the greatest discoveries in the history of astronomy was that the planets and stars move in fixed orbits. The three laws of planetary motion formulated by Johann Kepler in the early part of the seventeenth century mathematically demonstrated for the first time that heavenly bodies follow exact paths as they travel through space. These orbits are not approximate, but absolutely constant. Before Kepler, our knowledge of our universe was quite primitive and imprecise.

Kepler's feat was an outstanding early example of the combination of theoretical knowledge and empirical observations leading to the discovery of certain natural laws that exist in our universe. However, credit for the discovery of these laws of the fixed order of the stars and planets must go to another individual who lived 2,000 years before Kepler.

The prophet Jeremiah was told this amazing truth in the clearest language possible.

*Thus says the LORD, Who gives the sun for light by day,
and the fixed order of the moon and the stars for light by
night...*
Jeremiah 31:35

*Thus says the LORD, "If My covenant for day and night
stand not, and the fixed patterns of heaven and earth I
have not established, then I would reject the descendants
of Jacob and David My servant..."*
Jeremiah 33:25-26

The God who "in the beginning...created the heavens and the earth" (Genesis 1:1) also created and established the natural laws that govern the fixed order and movements of the heavenly bodies.

The predominant theory of how our universe came into existence is that 10 billion years ago a giant explosion took place, called the "Big Bang," bringing the universe into being. In essence we are told that our incredible orderly universe had its beginning in a state of high disorder: an explosion.

Imagine for a moment the following scenario: Take a giant object whose weight is approximately 6,000,000,000,000,000,000,000 tons. Now allow it to travel at the very high speed of 18.5 miles per second. Finally trace its yearly orbit around the sun for 365.26 days for the past 5,000 years, and the next 5,000 years. I think you will find that this giant mass, moving at such a high velocity, is our very own planet Earth. It took 365.26 days for it to make one complete orbit around our sun 5,000 years ago. 5,000 years from now, it also will travel its circuit around the sun in 365.26 days. What incredible order.

Leprosy And The Old Testament

S. I. McMillen stated that the word "leprosy" brought terror into the hearts of everyone. He stated:

> "For many hundreds of years the dreaded disease leprosy had killed countless millions of people in Europe." (19)

Even such scourges as the Black Death, which appeared in the fourteenth century and killed an estimated sixty million people, and syphilis, which began its reign of terror in the fifteenth century, could not elicit such a state of horrid frenzy in the hearts of people as leprosy.

By the fourteenth century it was reaping epidemic destruction in Europe and the greatest medical minds of Europe were at a loss to offer help in stemming the plague.

McMillen asked,

> "What did the physicians offer to stop the ever-increasing ravages of Leprosy? Some taught that it was 'brought on by eating hot food, pepper, garlic and the meat of diseased hogs.' Other physicians said it was caused by malign conjunction of the planets. Naturally, their suggestions for prevention were utterly worthless." (20)

The church, however, had a revolutionary concept that was clearly spoken about and found in the Old Testament book of Leviticus. As one reads Leviticus 13 the idea of contagion is brought out in detail along with the solution to the spread of infectious disease.

When a person was confirmed to have leprosy he was to be excluded and segregated from his community. Leviticus 13:46 states:

> *He shall remain unclean all the days during which he has the infection; he is unclean. He shall live alone; his dwelling shall be outside the camp.*

It must be remembered that while our doctors today know all about the concept of germs and contagious disease, a physician 500 to 1,000 years ago knew absolutely nothing, not even what a germ was.

The medical wisdom that the church found in the Holy Bible was the key to bringing the major plagues of the Dark Ages under control. If the church had not begun to implement the Biblical principles regarding contagious disease, who knows how many millions of additional lives would have been snuffed out during those plague-filled years?

Catching Up

Far from lagging behind the times, the Bible has always stood at the vanguard of scientific knowledge. We could have chosen many other examples from the fields of geology, biology, archaeology, anatomy and physics. In every one of these disciplines, the Holy Scriptures have proven scientifically accurate. Science has proven the Bible over and over again, not disproving it, as many have claimed.

The main focus of the Bible, however, is not in the realm of science. Its central theme is the love of God for humanity. It is a guidebook showing us how to live life to the fullest. But whenever it touches on matters of science and medicine, its data are always perfect, although it rarely attempts to scientifically prove the facts it presents. In fact, I believe that God may have intentionally left the proof of its scientific statements up to man, as a testimony to him of God's infinite foreknowledge and wisdom.

The problem with our leading technological minds is that they must have the answers to everything. Man's quest to know why and how things work and came into being is never ending.

God, however, tells us that there are many things we will never be able to prove, but must accept by faith. Hebrews 11:3 says:

> *By faith we understand that the worlds were prepared by the word of God, so that what is seen was not made out of things which are visible.*

Many of today's scientists cannot accept God because He can't be proven scientifically, yet they expect us to believe their theories on how the universe came into existence 10 billion years ago (the Big Bang) and how we as humans came about (evolution). Sadly "the Big Bang" and "evolution" are just that, theories, based on many assumptions, which, like God, must also be accepted on faith.

The study of origins boils down to a question of faith, either in God's word, the Bible, or in man's theories. To carry these two opposing viewpoints further, the fundamental question now becomes one of divine design versus chance occurrence.

Our entire lives are based on orderliness, purpose, meaning and reason. The Bible is a book that serves to strengthen all of these areas in our lives. It tells us where we came from. It explains why we are here. It describes where we are going and gives us the answers to many of life's deep questions. Science can only offer you the following scenario: You came into this world by blind chance and when you leave it you will go back into nothingness.

Science can offer us no hope when it comes to the question of origins or destinies. Even in its own field of expertise, describing how and why things work, it has only helped to validate what the Bible said all along, on numerous scientific discoveries as the previous examples have shown.

Perhaps you have never read the Bible because you were led to believe that it was an "old book" for "old people," with little relevance for you today. I hope that the preceding scientific discussion has served to whet your appetite. There just may be a bit more to the Bible than you may have thought or been told.

The Holy Scriptures have quite an impressive track record when they speak on scientific matters. What they said 2,000 years ago holds just as true now as it did then. Can we say the same thing about science? Our great scholars, professors and men of science want you to believe that you are the evolutionary product of a 2- to 4-billion-year process. Yet these same individuals can't tell you with certainty what the weather is going to be like on the next day. Can blind chance create magnificence? No, but the God of the Bible can.

The Institute For Creation Research

In southern California today we see a perfect example of science and the Bible finally meeting up and joining forces instead of doing battle. The Institute for Creation Research (ICR) is a research and educational organization of dozens of full-time or adjunct scientific faculty, many of whom hold Ph.D. degrees in a wide variety of scientific disciplines, and who believe that the Bible is fully accurate on all matters. They also believe that our earth and living systems are a product of intelligent creation and not of evolution.

The faculty at the ICR have written scores of books and numerous technical monographs presenting the latest scientific data supporting the concepts of creation and a young earth. (21)

Abortion: Science And The Bible Meet

When a sperm and an egg cell unite, a most unique and wonderful miracle occurs: life begins. This tiny single cell, no bigger than the period at the end of this sentence, now contains all the genetic materials needed to allow this most precious life to begin its journey through time.

This one cell, deep within its mysterious chambers, has the ability to divide and subdivide into over 100 trillion cells by the time it reaches adulthood. Over 6 billion of these 100 trillion cell packages exist today, each unique and yet alike. Each began in the same way: as one cell.

In America during the past 10 years, over 15 million of these little bundles have not been allowed to take their first breath, but have been terminated by "legal abortion."

The question of abortion is incredibly important, since it is now estimated that over 50 million of them are performed worldwide each year. A great proportion of the countries in our world, not just America, allow for legal abortions. If our definition of when life begins is wrong, then history will record our era as one of unprecedented genocide.

In 1973 the United States Supreme Court, in the Landmark *Roe v. Wade* decision, ruled that abortion was legal. The vote was seven to two in favor of legalization. Since then abortion has become the second most common surgical procedure (after circumcision) in our country.

U.S. Supreme Court Justice Blackmum reflected the thinking behind this monumental decision:

> "We need not resolve the difficult question of when life begins. When those trained in the respective disciplines of medicine, philosophy, and theology are unable to arrive at any consensus, the judiciary. . .is not in a position to speculate as to the answer." (22)

In 1857 our Supreme Court was also involved with another landmark case. By a six to three margin, the "highest court in the land" ruled that blacks were "non persons" (slaves), had no freedom, no civil rights and could be bought and sold as property at the will of their masters.

If our Supreme Court could have blundered so severely in the Dred Scott Case of 1857, could it also just be possible they made a mistake that has cost over 40 million lives?

The Bible has consistently taken its stand that life begins at conception. As one reads the Scriptures we can quickly see how God tells us of His plan for these precious little ones, including you and me.

Psalm 139:15-16 says,

> *My frame was not hidden from Thee, when I was made in secret, and skillfully wrought in the depths of the earth. Thine eyes have seen my unformed substance; and in Thy Book they were all written, the days that were ordained for me, when as yet there was not one of them.*

God knows all about us before we are even born. Listen to the words of the Lord as He spoke to the great prophet Jeremiah:

> *Before I formed you in the womb I knew you, and before you were born I consecrated you; I have appointed you a prophet to the nations.*
> Jeremiah 1:5

Concerning the miraculous birth of Jesus, we read:

> *And the angel said to her, "Do not be afraid, Mary; for you have found favor with God. And behold, you will conceive in your womb, and bear a son, and you shall name him Jesus."*
> Luke 1:30-31

As we study the Bible we can see that God tells us of the birth and exploits of many people before they are even born. The following list gives us some further examples:

Isaac	Genesis 17:19
Samson	Judges 13:3-5

| John the Baptist | Luke 1:13-17 |
| Samuel | I Samuel 1:10-20 |

For all of these men, at the moment of conception, the foreknowledge of God became the reality of life. From that point on, to have aborted these babies would have been to blot out the wonderful futures God had planned for them.

The great minds of medicine and science 100 years ago knew very little about fetal development. Justice Blackmun's statement about the lack of consensus between science and the Bible (theology) regarding the beginning of life, which we read earlier, may have been accurate in 1900, but it isn't accurate anymore.

Science tells us an incredible array of documented facts regarding early fetal development. A baby's heart starts beating from eighteen to twenty-five days after conception, usually before the mother even knows she is pregnant. By the thirtieth day, almost every organ has begun to form. By forty-four days, the brain waves are active and are identical to those of adults. At fifty-six days the baby has his own fingerprints, can make a fist and can urinate. At sixty days he can feel pain. By seventy-five days he is sensitive to heat, touch, light and noise.

Finally, by the end of twelve weeks (eighty-four days), which is the end of the first trimester of pregnancy, all body systems are working, even though the baby weighs only one ounce and is two to three inches long.

Science has shown us that all of this is happening in the first trimester. Yet in *Roe v. Wade* the U.S. Supreme Court ruled that during the first three months of pregnancy the decision to abort is left totally to the judgment of the woman and her attending physician.

At the turn of the twentieth century, science could only tell us that at the twelfth week of pregnancy a "wad of cells" existed. Today, embryologists tell us that at twelve weeks what we have is a perfectly formed tiny human being. There is perfect consensus between the Bible and science that at three months life has not only begun but is complete and thriving.

Many scientists argue that, if a person is in a coma and on artificial life support systems, as long as he has brain activity he is alive. If this is so then science has placed the time of the beginning of life at forty-

47

four days (six to seven weeks), since this is when a baby has brain waves identical to those of that same person in a coma.

What if we view the beating of a human heart as our barometer for life? Since most people today equate heart attacks, and the cessation of the functioning of the heart, with death, then at eighteen to twenty-five days (three weeks) our little pre-born (newborn) is clearly alive. Since most women do not even know they are pregnant at three weeks, abortion is not even an option yet.

But what is happening in that initial period between conception and three weeks? We see a fantastic growth in the birth and development of cells. Life is exploding on the scene. The only conclusion from the study of science and the Bible is that both have proven that a consensus does indeed exist, regardless of what the Supreme Court may say, that life begins at conception. Once again science has caught up to what the Bible said 2,000 years ago.

Medical technology has also been given the privilege to show us that the concept of viability (the ability for the baby to live outside the mother's womb with special medical care in most cases before the normal nine months' gestation is complete) is constantly changing. And as it does, it is bringing us closer to when the Bible says life begins.

According to the U.S. Supreme Court (even in *Roe v. Wade*), viability is an important consideration as to when life begins. The answer to this question, however, depends on when you were born. Back in 1850 even babies born at eight months (one month premature) had a low survival rate. By 1930, thanks to medical advances, birth at seven months offered a good chance for survival. By 1950, six months became the dividing line. 1970's five-month babies are now happy and healthy young adults. Today there are babies prematurely born as early as four and one half months who are alive and perfectly healthy.

By 2020, we may be down to three months; by 2040 we may be down to two months, etc. The Bible once again has proven itself to be a book that has not only the answers to much of our difficult scientific questions but to the social ones also.

The Ultimate Textbook

In almost any field of science we literally have to completely rewrite all textbooks every 100 years. Biology, chemistry and physics textbooks from our great scholars of 1800 have little value in explaining our complex universe today. They are so full of errors and their gaps in knowledge so wide, they would be laughed out of even a present-day high school classroom.

The Bible for over 2,000 years has undergone absolutely no revisions yet is far from being outdated. It is totally accurate on all scientific matters in our ultra-high-tech, space-age world. Its claims are amazing, its accuracy incredible. The challenge to view its contents presents the reader with a most wonderful opportunity to explore a book like no other book ever written.

Chapter 5
Time–The Amazing Dimension

Time. This most precious, mysterious and universal of all concepts has fascinated mankind since its beginning. From the moment of conception, our odyssey through time begins. Please travel with me as I attempt to unravel some of the mysteries of this most amazing dimension and the profound influence the Bible has had in arranging and affecting how we utilize it in our daily lives.

The first thing we notice about the dimension of time is that it can be broken down into many different intervals. The average American today can expect to live to approximately seventy years of age. This is the equivalent of 840 months, 3,640 weeks, 25,550 days, 613,200 hours, 36,792,000 minutes or 2,207,520,000 seconds.

Time can also be sliced in many other interesting ways. For example, if we sleep an average of eight hours a day, then fully one-third of our existence is spent asleep. Of the 25,550 days our life consists of (if we live to the average of seventy years), we are left with only 17,033 days of activity time. This is because our sleep time is used for complete body rest. 17,033 days doesn't seem all that much, but one thing is certain, by the time you read this chapter and wake up the next day, one less day will be in your reserve.

But all of these above figures are averages. The allotment of days each one of you reading this book has left to live will vary substantially. If we measure time in terms of activity days left to live (that is, days measured in terms of waking hours) the following chart gives you a picture of how many more days we have left on this planet, assuming we live to be seventy.

CURRENT AGE	DAYS LEFT TO LIVE
10	14,598
20	12,165
30	9,732
40	7,299
50	4,866
55	3,650
60	2,433
65	1,216

As we get older, how little precious time we seem to have left. With such little time available to us, the question of how best to use what we have, and to find some meaning in life as out days rapidly dwindle, becomes of paramount importance.

The Bible has some very special ideas on how to best utilize our time here on earth. Many people, however, have shied away from reading the Bible because they feel it is out of date and behind the times. For an old book, the Bible has left behind it a legacy of unparalleled influence with respect to how we view and use time. May the following observations allow you to decide for yourself just how "timely" the Bible really is.

The Twenty-first Century

As we stand in time at the very beginning of our third millennium it's fun to reflect back at all the fanfare that greeted the coming of year 2000. Many other famous years have become permanently placed in your memory, such as 1492 (Columbus discovered America), 1776 (America became an independent nation) and the year you were born.

Just who is responsible for setting up the yearly dating scheme that has become almost universally adopted today? The monk Dionysius Exiguus, in the sixth century after Christ, established what is commonly referred to as the Christian era. He placed Jesus' birth on December 25 in the year 753 of Rome and decided 754 should be the first year of the Christian era, i.e., A.D. 1. (23). The initials B.C. mark the years before the beginning of the Christian era and stand for "Before Christ"; A.D. represents Anno Domini – "in the year of our Lord."

One man's birth is responsible for the beginning of our modern era and how we measure all of our great historical dates. Jesus Christ, the central person of the New Testament, can be viewed as the great timepiece, standing at the crossroads between our ancient and modern eras. During the year A.D. 2000 we had to acknowledge his birth and the fact that we were living in the 2000th year of our Lord." His influence cannot be ignored.

Christmas Time

There is absolutely no day during the year that can generate such excitement and such business as December 25. Even though Santa Claus, the Christmas tree, gift giving and all the other trappings are important parts of the celebration, the central theme and reason for this special day centers around the birth of Jesus. The birth of Christ ushered in not only the Christian era but the most influential single day in American society each year.

Weeks and even months before December 25 arrives all the major department stores across our country have countdown days till Christmas. This certainly makes good business sense when you figure that we as Americans spend many billions each year on over 2 billion gifts. For many businesses, over 25% of their annual income is generated by sales related to the Christmas season. A poor Christmas season can literally send our economy into a tailspin. Strange how the birth of a tiny baby boy 2,000 years ago can have such a profound effect on our economy today; but He does.

In addition to the incredible amount of gifts we exchange each year, almost $1 billion will be spent each season on Christmas cards. And Christmas stamps and Christmas seals are as American as baseball and apple pie. Many millions of people spend hours on end addressing, writing and mailing their cards each year. The avalanche of cards and gifts is so great that our postal service warns us to mail them days and even weeks in advance to insure prompt delivery. Our faithful postmen are taxed to the fullest by the cards alone.

Another fascinating sociological effect the Christmas season has is to generate a special warmth and spirit of brotherly love throughout our land for the entire month of December. During this month our radio stations begin to serenade us with those wonderful Christmas carols and songs that make this season so special. Our television sets are also bombarded with Christmas specials galore. Every variety show is also guaranteed to have a yearly Christmas extravaganza.

More smiles are seen from our normally sad faces during the Christmas season than at any other time. More well wishes are given by more people than at any other time of year. It's like no other part of the year—where good tidings and good cheer become the norm rather than the exception.

Sadly, the central reason for this wonderful bustle of activity and warm heartedness is usually placed in the background. The birth of Jesus is clearly the reason for the season, but the manger scene is often overwhelmed not by the spirit of giving but by the spirit of indulgence. Yet the Bible is still the driving catalyst, 2,000 years after one of its recorded events (the birth of Jesus), behind the most influential day in our culture.

Time Off

If we were to take a poll of New York City public school children, asking them what their favorite book is, few would probably say the Bible. If we were to tell this same group of youngsters that this same book is responsible for many of the holidays they have off during the school year, they just might find themselves a new favorite book.

The largest public school system in our country is located in New York City. Each year, in addition to a two-month summer vacation, these students enjoy many holidays off. During a typical school year seven major holidays are allocated to the students and teachers due to the celebration of events surrounding God and the Bible.

These seven holidays which are centered around various aspects of the Bible and God are:

ROSH HASHANAH is another name for the Jewish New Year. It ushers in a ten-day period of self-examination and penitence for the Jewish people. During this time Jewish people all over the world reflect on their relationship with God. In addition, Jews also celebrate and commemorate the creation of the world and the establishment of the Jewish nation from the father of the Jews, Abraham. The Book of Genesis describes in detail how the Jews became God's chosen people.

YOM KIPPUR is the most important holiday of the Jewish year. It is the Jewish "Day of Atonement." It is a day that Jews fast and set aside to "afflict the soul," to atone for the sins of the past year.

THANKSGIVING is the special day the Pilgrims set apart in 1621 when they gave public thanks to God for their good harvests and general blessings. The Pilgrims were deeply religious people who came to America to build a government based on the Bible.

CHRISTMAS is known worldwide as a joyful holiday celebrating the birth of Jesus Christ. While its origin is pagan and not biblical, no holiday in our modern world is given such fanfare and general good cheer as Christmas. Its influence is so astounding that we refer to it as the Christmas season.

GOOD FRIDAY is when the crucifixion of Jesus Christ is commemorated. It is a very special day for Christians worldwide and many special church services are held on that day.

PASSOVER is a Hebrew festival commemorating the sparing of the lives of the Hebrew children when the destroying angel slew the first-born in Egypt. It marks the liberation of the Jewish people from their bondage in Egypt. You can read the full account of the institution of Passover in Exodus 12.

EASTER commemorates the resurrection of Jesus Christ on the third day after His crucifixion, death and burial. Its institution as a tribute to Jesus Christ is now celebrated worldwide.

It is kind of ironic how our United States Supreme Court has ruled prayer in our schools unconstitutional, yet many of the New York City public school holidays are attributed to a book that is all about prayer: the Bible.

The Week

Everyone knows that a week is a period of time that consists of seven days. But perhaps you have never realized or thought about the fact that the week is the only important time marker in human life that is not clearly based on an astronomical foundation. The day, month, year and seasons are all based on the earth's rotation, orbit, tilt and relation to the moon and sun. For example, the duration of one orbit of the earth around the sun represents one year.

How the week came into being is something most encyclopedias treat very superficially. They all acknowledge that they do not know exactly how this duration of time came into existence. Some encyclopedias suggest that the origin of the week revolved around business or market days, which were usually six, seven, or eight days in length. Others say that the Sumerians and Babylonians may have originated the concept by dividing the year into weeks of seven days each, with one day reserved for recreation.

Most discussions about the origin of the week, however, acknowledge that its first use was by the ancient Hebrews. Their observance of it was based on the Genesis account of creation. The biblical account states that God created the world in six days and that on the seventh He rested. Genesis 1 and 2 give us a very detailed description of what God created on each one of those first six days.

As Henry Morris stated so well:

> "Every effect must have an adequate cause, and the only cause which is truly able to account for such a remarkable phenomenon as the week is that it was established at creation and has been deeply etched in the common human consiciousness ever since." (24)

Universal Time

People in general live their lives by the clock. We set our clock to wake us up in the morning. We watch our clocks to tell us when to eat lunch and dinner. Our clocks and calendars tell us what time and what day our favorite television shows are on. We plan weddings a year in advance. We even time how long it takes to run a race, travel from one place to another, and the interval between labor pains.

What makes it possible for us to measure time, and use it as such a reliable yardstick in all our daily affairs, is its amazing quality of exactness. Our universe is arranged in a fantastic, orderly manner. So orderly is our entire universe that time measurement becomes a reality to us as a by-product of this orderliness. The movements of our universe provide us with our concepts of time.

The two principal time markers, the year and the day, are universally accepted and used throughout our world. As we stated earlier, the year is the duration of one orbital revolution of the earth about the sun and is 365.26 days in length. The day is the duration of one rotation of the earth on its axis and is equal to twenty-four hours. These movements of our earth are so constant and exacting that they give us the ability to map time out in a perfect and precise fashion.

Our earth's orbit is so certain and unchanging that we can predict exactly where our planet will be in our solar system at any given time. In relation to the sun we know that in 365.26 days our planet will be exactly where it is now. The reason for this precise accuracy and consistency is that our universe is governed by physical laws that never change. Without this orderliness, time could not be what we know of today, but something quite different.

To further illustrate how our universe is so amazing, consider the following: Our moon is constantly revolving around our earth day after day, year after year, century after century in an exact orbit. Our earth in turn, along with its moon, is orbiting our sun year after year, century after century also in a perfect orbit. Our sun, scientists tells us, along with all of its planets and their respective moons, is traveling at a speed of 600,000 miles per hour in a gigantic orbit through its galaxy, an orbit that requires over 2 million centuries to complete. Scientists also believe that our entire Milky Way Galaxy is also moving with respect to other galaxies; and so it goes.

What we have is trillions upon trillions of heavenly bodies, weighing trillions upon trillions of tons moving at very high velocities (eighteen miles per second and faster) in exact orbits in relation to one another and never colliding. This orderliness defies human comprehension. We as human beings, with such rational, orderly and ingenious minds, have trouble walking a straight line, yet these heavenly hosts can move through our universe with such exquisite grace and perfect form that they appear to have minds of their own.

How is this possible? We only have two choices to explain these movements. One choice is the so-called scientific explanation. Briefly, this option states that one day there existed absolutely nothing in the universe. Then, in the course of time, out of this nothingness an incredible amount of matter came into existence (all the matter that is in our universe today). Its form was originally some type of gigantic blob of materials that somehow, by itself, either exploded or gradually broke up into the incredible, complex and orderly universe we have today. To sum up: we started with nothing, and nothing by itself became everything. In turn everything, by itself, developed into perfection; and all of this was guided by blind chance.

The second choice is from the Bible. Genesis 1:1 states, "In the beginning God created the heavens and the earth." And Genesis 1:16 declares, "And God made the two great lights, the greater light to govern the day, and lesser light to govern the night; He made the stars also." God created the universe and established its order.

Neither of the above choices can be proved in the normal scientific way, which is through observable, repeatable experimentation. Since this is a question of origins, by its very nature, one of the above two choices must be accepted by faith. It would seem that the first choice would require a far greater degree of faith then the second one. When you place your trust in the first option you are faced with the inevitable conclusion that you came from nothing and that when you die you are going back to nothing. In between, you, on the average, will experience seventy or eighty perfectly accurate and constant units of time called years to find some kind of meaning. The latter choice has a book—the Bible—containing almost 750,000 words explaining why there just might be a better way.

Beginnings And Endings

Time is a continuum. And it has a past, a present and future. The present is easy to understand because we live our entire lives in that dimension. The past and the future are concepts that are also simple to describe and understand. However, the farther back we go into the past and the further we venture into the future, our memories, concepts and visions begin to fade. Finally, the question of when our universe began, if indeed it had a beginning, and when it will all end, if it ever will, become questions that our finite minds can't comprehend. The idea of infinity, by its very nature, is beyond our thinking capacity.

Although our rational minds can't truly comprehend the great time scope of our universe, it hasn't stopped us from spending a great deal of our time pondering this most intriguing of all human questions. The

American Heritage Dictionary defines eternity as "The totality of time without beginning or end." (25) It also defines infinite as "Continuing endlessly in time." (26) While written information on beginnings and endings, eternity and infinity is very sparse and sketchy at best, the Bible has quite a bit to say on this subject.

Even our great modern scientific minds can at best theorize that our universe may have begun 10 to 15 billion years ago in a whirlwind of activity that saw a cataclysmic explosion propel our universe into existence. Yet they have little to offer us regarding where the original matter came from. Clearly, if they have such difficulty in explaining when everything began, they have even a harder time in telling us when and if things will ever end.

No book in the history of mankind has had more impact on our world with respect to how we view time than the Bible. No book has had more influence in every area of our lives today than the Bible. Even the most prestigious encyclopedia in the world, the *Encyclopedia Britannica,* acknowledges this awesome impact by devoting over 100 pages to discussing this one book. Not only has the Bible established how we keep time, not only has it helped describe our history throughout time, but it has proven itself to stand the test of time by being a book that is timeless.

With credentials such as these, when the Holy Scriptures speak regarding beginnings and endings, at the very least our curiosity should be stirred to examine what they have to say on the subject. The name of the very first book of the Bible, Genesis, means "coming into being, origin." The first chapter of this first book of the Bible gives us a very detailed account of how the universe, day and night, the planets and animals, the ground and water and man were created. Genesis 1 has been analyzed and debated, and has enchanted and fascinated mankind, more than any other chapter ever written.

Its beauty of presentation is undeniable. Its explanation of how our universe and world began is simple but profound. Even its plausibility is far more appealing than that of the "so-called" scientific explanation we just explored. If you have never read this remarkable chapter, you owe it to yourself to do so.

What happens to someone at death? This single question has preoccupied our minds more than any other. It is only appropriate that the Bible addresses this issue at great length. In fact, the New Testament mentions eternal life and everlasting life over forty times. If the question of what happens to you when you die is something that interests you, perhaps the Bible can present you with some thoughts and insights into the matter. By the time you finish reading this book, approximately 1 million people will have passed into eternity. At the moment of their departure into this dimension, where they will spend eternity becomes the only question on their minds. Again, before you are ready to take your leap into eternity, you owe it to yourself to explore the most provocative and exhaustive exposition of eternal life ever written.

Worship Time

Mention the word "Sunday" and many people will immediately think of football games, sleeping late, a day off from work and even going to church. From its very inception as a nation, America has always been a society of churchgoers. Throughout our great country, Sunday is known to all who regularly attend church as well as to those who do not as the day to worship God. The Bible has by far been America's book of worship to God. Its message and words of wisdom, praise and love are responsible for sending tens of millions of our citizens to church on Sunday mornings.

No single book has been able to consistently bring out more people in America and, for that matter, around the world for one singular activity, worship, than any other ever written. Sunday is the time when the Holy Scriptures become the center of attraction for millions of people throughout the world. Since the days of Jesus, almost 100,000 Sundays have come and gone. Yet the worship of God is still generating the largest crowds of any single regular activity of all time.

Time To Think

Time is our most precious resource in many senses. For one thing, our reserves are constantly being depleted. Secondly, we never know when our allotment of time will come to an end. Thirdly, there is no way to obtain or buy more for oneself. And finally, time lost can never be found again. With these factors in mind, how we best manage and maximize the use of the time we have here on earth has to be considered a critical priority in all of our lives.

As one ponders this very provocative and important concept, one must be impressed with just how precious little time we have to live, in comparison with the eternity of our universe. 3,000 to 5,000 more days left to live can be quite a disheartening thing, especially when you know that your health most likely will continue to decline throughout the remainder of your life.

The Bible, from both its internal witness and from external evidence, has proven to be a book of incredible beauty, insight and influence to generation after generation with respect to this most intriguing concept of time.

Its internal witness has fascinated mankind along all avenues of time. Its incomparable account of the beginning of time, space, matter and life as told in Genesis 1 is full of beauty, mystery and plausibility. No one can truly say they have pondered all the alternatives to creation without reading its account. Eternal life, the most sought-after dream of every human being who has ever lived, is graphically explored, explained and visually depicted for us throughout the New Testament. The romantic in all of us should long to examine this portal in time. Finally, the great bulk of the Bible is devoted to giving out advice on how to best utilize these 25,000 days of life we have to live.

The external evidence is all around us today for anyone who takes the time to look. The way we view time is just another by-product of this 2,000-year-old book.

The time has come for us to reexamine our place in time and eternity and allow ourselves the rare privilege to journey into the pages of the world of "Father Time," the God of the Bible.

Chapter 6
Tylenol And The Bible

This at first may seem like a strange title for a chapter in a book about the Bible, but let me explain. During the early 1980's, the Tylenol scare swept across our nation. Several people died as a result of taking Tylenol capsules that were laced with cyanide. Since that one incident, a dramatic change has taken place in our entire medicine and food industry. Over-the-counter (nonprescription) capsules are almost gone, replaced with tablets, pills and caplets. And many medications and now foods are being specially packaged with safety seals and other tamper-resistant devices.

The damage to Tylenol sales and its reputation was great indeed due to this unfortunate event. The usefulness of Tylenol as a pain reliever and fever reducer is of unquestionable value. Yet it took a great deal of expensive special advertising to restore public confidence in this wonder drug. Tylenol was the victim of a great deal of unwarranted bad press. But because of its intrinsic beneficial nature to mankind, it was able to survive the scare it underwent. Today Tylenol sales are tremendous.

The same kind of unwarranted "bad press" has been leveled against the Hold Scriptures more than once throughout their long history. They have been attacked, criticized, assailed, mocked and even dismissed by many groups of people and from every angle you can possibly imagine.

People down through the ages have stated that the Bible is not historical and is full of errors in the realm of history. Critics have long contended that the Bible is a dull book for old people. It has been called a crutch that people turn to in times of trouble. Many of our leading scientists view a belief in this book as impossible based on what our science tells us today. You can't believe in science and the Bible at the same time, they tell us. From being labeled outdated to outlandish, from faulty to foolish, the Bible has been the recipient of a great deal of bad press.

The challenges that have been hurled at God's Word must now be addressed. In return, I would like to throw a challenge or two back to these detractors, and allow you to weigh and examine the evidence for yourself.

Challenge 1—It Isn't Historical

Back in 1955 a German journalist named Werner Keller wrote a book called *The Bible As History*. In the closing words of his introduction Mr. Keller stated:

> "In view of the overwhelming mass of authentic and well-attested evidence now available, as I thought of the skeptical criticism which from the eighteenth century onwards would fain have demolished the Bible altogether, there kept hammering on my brain this one sentence: 'The Bible is right after all.' " (27)

Since then, this book has sold over 10 million copies. Few non-fiction books ever reach this amazing sales plateau. Yet when Mr. Keller combined the subject of the Bible, the discipline of history, and his wonderful journalistic flair the result became a phenomenal best-seller of intrigue, adventure, excitement and biblical history.

Many critics of the Holy Scriptures consider the Bible to be a book full of errors in all fields (including historical matters), and nothing more than a book of fables, legends and stories written and rewritten many times. For a book that claims to be written under the inspiration of God, to contain many historical errors would certainly lessen its credibility. The exciting thing, however, is that our twentieth-century archaeologists have been able, through diligent scientific research and methods, to validate countless biblical narratives as irrefutable and historically accurate.

One hundred years ago biblical critics were quick to level scathing attacks on the Bible. They stated that many of its accounts of people and places could only be found in the pages of the Bible itself and nowhere else. They contended that these accounts couldn't be true because they couldn't find any other historical information from any other sources to corroborate what the Bible said. Based on this line of reasoning these skeptics proudly boasted that the Bible was full of historical discrepancies. Since that time the archaeologist has entered the scene and has decisively put to rest the belief that the Bible is not a true book of history.

Just exactly what is an archaeologist? Howard Vos stated,

> "To many, an archaeologist is a morbid creature who enjoys poking around ancient ruins to discover dead men's bones, bits of pottery, weapons, or tools. Such an idea is far from the truth. Rather, he is something of a scientist, whether amateur or professional; and he interests himself in a study of dead things only as a means of learning about the life of an ancient people... His knowledge is acquired by systematic observation or study, and facts discovered are evaluated and classified into an organized body of information. Moreover, archaeology is a composite science because it seeks assistance from many other sciences." (28)

Science has once again come to the aid of validating the Bible, and this time it is in the area of history. The following are just a few examples of how our modern archaeological discoveries have confirmed the historical accuracy of our ancient Bible.

Sargon

> "according to Robert Dick Wilson, the names of twenty-six foreign kings recorded in the Old Testament have been found on documents contemporary with the kings. In addition, the names of six kings of Israel and four of Judah have been located in Assyrian records."

This was from the 1926 publication of Wilson's book *A Scientific Investigation of the Old Testament*. Since then the number has grown to about fifty. (29)

Keller provided us with an example of the evidence of one of those kings:

> "The French vice-consul in Mosul, Paul-Emile Botta, was an enthusiastic archaeologist. In 1843 He began to dig at Khorsabad on the Tigris and from the ruins of a 4,000-year-old capital proudly brought to light the first witness to the Bible: Sargon, the fabulous ruler of Assyria." (30)

Isaiah 20:1 states, "In the year that the commander came to Ashdod, when Sargon the King of Assyria sent him and he fought against Ashdod and captured it . . ." Zeus, Hercules, Apollo and Poseidon are all well-known names in Greek mythology. Each has a colorful past, but no reality. The kings of the Bible have an equally interesting past, but their reality is a fact of history. They were men of flesh and bones, not the product of ancient imagination as the Greek gods were.

Nineveh

The story of Jonah and the whale may be familiar to many people who do not even read the Bible. Jonah was a great prophet of the Lord. He was commissioned by God to warn a great city of ancient times to repent of her wickedness. We read about this mission in Jonah 1:2, when God told Jonah, "Arise, go to Nineveh the great city, and cry against it, for their wickedness has come up before Me." Jonah at first disobeyed, "And the LORD appointed a great fish to swallow Jonah, and Jonah was in the stomach of the fish three days and three nights" (Jonah 1:17).

Nineveh was one of the greatest cities of the ancient world. It was the Assyrian capital, known throughout the Bible for its great wickedness. It fell in 612 B.C. to the combined forces of the Medes, Babylonians and Scythians. From that point on Nineveh disappeared from history and its location was not discovered again until 1847, by Henry Layard. (31)

The significance of the discovery of Nineveh is truly monumental. First of all, over 25,000 clay tablets were unearthed from the fabulous royal library of King Ashurbanipal (668-626 B.C.), which was one of the most important libraries of the ancient world.

Secondly, as Keller stated,

> "They contained the essential material for under-standing the historical and intellectual background of Mesopotamia, its peoples, its kingdoms with their arts and crafts, cultures and religions. Among them were the Sumerian flood story and the Epic of Gilgamesh. What had been until then a mysterious sealed chapter of our world's history was suddenly opened and page after page was turned over. Rulers, cities, wars and stories which people had only heard about through the Old Testament revealed themselves as real facts." (32)

Thirdly, and perhaps the most significant facet of the Nineveh find and excavation, was how the Bible played an instrumental part in its discovery. For if it were not for the Bible and its mentioning the city of Nineveh, we probably would never have sought to find her, because we would have no idea that such a city existed. In the case of Nineveh, the great wealth of information we learned about ancient Mesopotamia might never have come to light if it were not for our Bible. So much of our knowledge of the history of the ancient Middle East exists today due to the very diligent efforts of archaeology. But much of the credit behind the scenes has to go to the Bible, for the Bible gave the archaeologist the clues on what to look for and where to look for it. The archaeological excavations have proven the Bible to be historically accurate. In addition, this one amazing book has itself been the guiding light illuminating the pathway for discovery after discovery into the fabulous mysteries of our ancient history.

Abraham

Abraham. The very name transcends time as well as continents. According to the *Encyclopedia Britannica*, Abraham was the "First of the Hebrew patriarchs and a figure revered by the three great monotheistic religions: Judaism, Christianity, and Islam." (33) He is commonly referred to as the father of the Jewish nation. Until the twentieth century, many felt that Abraham was a product of people's imagination. Many thought that he was nothing more than a legend, found only in the book of Genesis and elsewhere throughout the Bible.

In 1933 an extraordinary excavation began in the Middle East that far exceeded the greatest expectations of its excavators. The incredible journey into the "Kingdom of Mari" reads like a romantic, mystical tale of adventure. It would eventually yield a palace of over 200 rooms and courtyards and 24,000 tablets that described in great detail the fabulous civilization of Mari.

Science, detective work and an unquenchable thirst for knowledge all came to bear as the archaeologists slowly began to piece together the puzzle of this lost civilization. What emerged after years of excavation and thousands of hours of deciphering and translation of the tablets into our language of today was that Mari was a highly advanced culture existing 4,000 years ago. Industry, government, arts, crafts and writing were highly developed in this society.

The Mari expeditions, while greatly enriching our knowledge of ancient Mesopotamia, also gave us documents that in the words of Keller,

> ". . .Produce startling proof that the stories of the patriarchs in the Bible are not "pious legends" – as is often too readily assumed – but things that are described as happening in a historical period which can be precisely dated." (34)

Throughout the entire Mari excavations name after name of biblical cities heretofore only mentioned in the Bible came to life. Such cities as Haran and Nahor were found on inscriptions. Again Keller stated,

> "Haran, the home of Abraham, father of the patriarchs, the birthplace of the Hebrew people, is here for the first time historically attested, for contemporary texts refer to it." (35)

In addition, many names of people who played an important part in the Genesis account of patriarchal succession up to Abraham are specifically mentioned on various artifacts; and they date from the period that the Bible assigns to Abraham.

The Bible Is History

As the above examples show, our modern scholars have beyond a shadow of a doubt established the Bible as the most complete, extensive and authoritative book on ancient history available anywhere. There are countless other archaeological digs that have verified the accuracy of innumerable biblical accounts, accounts that are found only in the Bible, through their scientific and scholarly research. I dare say that the future should provide us with even more startling finds that corroborate the biblical narratives.

Is the Bible historically accurate? Perhaps a better question would be: How long will it take our archaeologists to discover further artifacts, tablets, statues and cities that will allow them to classify their finds as history, again confirming the words of the Bible? To phrase it differently, why not just accept the biblical account of history even where there is no other historical evidence, since the Bible's track record is so convincing? History and the Bible, far from being at opposite poles, are in reality mirror images reflecting the fact that "God's Word is history."

Challenge 2—You Can't Be A Scientist And Really Believe The Bible

The prevailing view today is that once a man or woman dedicates his or her life to scientific pursuits, he or she can no longer seriously believe in a literal interpretation of the Bible. When Charles Darwin's book *The Origin of Species* came out in 1859, a revolution in scientific thinking began that heralded the age of evolution. Darwin's influence on our way of thinking in our present age is truly monumental. His theory, many scientists contend, makes it not only unnecessary to believe in the Bible but foolish indeed.

Many of you may never have heard of Robert Boyle. But if I were to tell you that he is generally considered to be the father of modern chemistry, you might just be able to grasp his importance. Boyle (1627-1691), in addition to being a great scientist, was a strong believer in the Bible. His belief in the Word of God was so strong that he used a lot of his own money for Bible translation work. He apparently saw no conflict between being a man of science and a believer in the Holy Scriptures.

As one studies the private lives of many of the greatest scientists our world has produced during the last 500 years, he will be amazed at how many of them not only read the Bible but interpreted it literally, and used it as a guidebook for their lives.

The list of Bible-believing scientists reads like a "Who's Who" of the world of science. Names like Leonardo da Vinci, Isaac Newton, Louis Pasteur, Samuel Morse and Benjamin Franklin are known by scientists and laymen alike. Many other names are also universally known by scientist and science student. Individuals such as Kepler, Pascal, Faraday, Maxwell, Dalton, Joule, Kelvin, Fleming, Babbage, Carver and von Braun were all men who, in addition to being scientific geniuses, were also men who made the Bible the most important book in their own personal lives.

A sampling of the scientific disciplines these men and others are generally considered to be the founder or father of follows: (36)

SCIENTIST		DISCIPLINE
Leonardo da Vinci	(1452-1519)	Modern Science
Johann Kepler	(1571-1630)	Physical Astronomy
Blaise Pascal	(1623-1662)	Hydrostatics
Robert Boyle	(1627-1691)	Modern Chemistry
Isaac Newton	(1642-1727)	Calculus
John Dalton	(1766-1844)	Modern Atomic Theory
Georges Cuvier	(1769-1832)	Comparative Anatomy
Charles Babbage	(1792-1871)	Computer Science
Matthew Maury	(1806-1873)	Oceanography
James Joule	(1818-1889)	Thermodynamics
John A. Fleming	(1849-1945)	Electronics

In addition, these and other Bible-believing scientists formulated a host of universal natural laws that form the basic building blocks on which all of our science rests. The listing below highlights these laws and their discoverers:

DISCOVERER		LAW
Johann Kepler	(1571-1630)	Three laws of planetary motion
Robert Boyle	(1627-1691)	Basic laws relating gas pressure to temperature and volume
Isaac Newton	(1642-1727)	Law of universal gravitation. Basic three laws of motion
John Dalton	(1766-1844)	Gas law of partial pressures
Lord Kelvin	(1824-1907)	First and second laws of thermodynamics

As a few examples of just how influential the Bible was in these great men's lives, consider the following:

Lord Kelvin (1824-1907) was elected at the age of twenty-two as Glasgow University's youngest professor ever. It was his habit to open every one to his lectures with prayer.

Samuel Morse (1791-1872), who invented the telegraph in 1844, used a quote from the Bible for his first message: "What has God wrought." (Numbers 23:23 KJV)

Michael Faraday (1791-1867), who is without a doubt one of the greatest physicists of all time, was also a very humble man of God. At the age of fifty he became an elder in the Chapel Meeting House in Pauls Alley, London. He preached there every Sunday. Near his death he was quoted as saying,

> "My worldly faculties are slipping away day by day. Happy it is for all of us that the true good does not lie in them. As they ebb, may they leave us as little children trusting in the Father of Mercies and accepting His unspeakable gift. I bow before Him who is Lord of all." (37)

Isaac Newton (1642-1727), who many consider, along with Albert Einstein, one of the two greatest scientists who ever lived, is commonly know for sitting under a tree and having an apple fall on his head. This in turn led him to the discovery of the law of gravity. He was also credited with the development of calculus, formulating the universal laws stated earlier, establishing the particle theory of light propagation and many other monumental breakthroughs. This remarkable genius was quoted as saying,

> "We account the Scriptures of God to be the most sublime philosophy. I find more sure marks of authenticity in the Bible than in any profane history whatsoever." (38)

Finally, Wernher von Braun (1912-1977) was a great German space scientist. Later in life, after he became a U.S. citizen, he directed the U.S. guided-missile program and then became the Director of NASA. Always in the vanguard of the latest advances in space technology, von Braun once commented:

> "Manned space flight is an amazing achievement, but it has opened for mankind thus far only a tiny door for viewing the awesome reaches of space. An outlook through this peephole at the vast mysteries of the universe should only confirm our belief in the certainty of its Creator. I find it as difficult to understand a scientist who does not acknowledge the presence of a superior rationality behind the existence of the universe as it is to comprehend a theologian who would deny the advances of science." (39)

Johann Kepler (1571-1630), the great German astronomer, summed it up best, as he was exploring the vast reaches of the universe, by saying that he was "Thinking God's thoughts after Him."

It is important to note that a person's personal convictions and beliefs are an integral part of his very being. These values, by their very nature, are carried by an individual into every area of life, including his or her occupation. The scientists we have just listed were men who literally changed our world. Their discoveries and breakthroughs are now legendary. These men, however, all had one common denominator: They believed in and read the Bible. They undoubtedly used the wisdom gained from these sacred pages to help them unlock the great mysteries of our natural world, thereby changing the course of history forever.

We owe a great debt to these pioneers of yesteryear. The scientists of today who have problems in finding the Bible hard to reconcile with the precise, concrete and rational realm of the scientific disciplines would do well to consider the backgrounds of many scientific predecessors. For these were the men whom laid the very foundations of the modern fields of research. Perhaps if they realized how integral a role the Bible played in these geniuses' lives and work, they just might reconsider reading this old book. Can a scientist believe in the Bible? History shows that not only can he, but he has. Genius, discovery and the Bible have long been companions in the quest for knowledge.

Challenge 3—It's A Crutch

If you have ever broken your leg, you probably have had to use crutches to get around. A crutch is an aid. In its broadest sense it is anything that is depended upon for support. It can be something physical, as in the case of the wooden crutches used to help you walk when you break a leg or ankle. It can be chemical. Alcohol, cigarettes and drugs are heavily relied upon by millions to help get them through the day. Finally, it can be psychological. Many people watch television so much that they are in a sense addicted to the tube. Studies have shown that people actually suffer withdrawal symptoms if they are away from their T.V. sets too long. And yes, many say that the Bible and God are a crutch people turn to in order to help them cope with their daily struggles.

What Do Others Have to Say About The Bible?

Ulysses S. Grant, our eighteenth president, considered the Bible to be a book needed to provide our nation with support when he said:

"Hold fast to the Bible as the sheet-anchor of your liberties. Write its precepts in your hearts and practice them in your lives." (40)

Benjamin Franklin also understood how important a good support system is when he remarked,

"A Bible and a newspaper in every house, a good school in every district – all studied and appreciated as they merit – are the principal support of virtue, morality and civil liberty." (41)

Helen Keller, although she spent almost her entire life deaf and without sight, became a symbol to the entire world of the unlimited potential the human spirit possesses to overcome personal trials and handicaps. To this incredible woman, being deaf, mute and blind, only propelled her on to greatness. She was the author of nine books, graduated from Radcliffe College with honors, contributed $2 million to a foundation to help others and once remarked, "The Bible is one mighty representative of the whole spiritual life of humanity." (42)

These people and countless millions of others have down through the centuries understood that in our world, where the struggle to survive is so ever present, the Bible has always been a sure rock on which they could depend. Wisdom, insights, soothing words, purpose and so much more have always been woven into the pages of this timeless book. Character building, integrity, honesty, loving and giving are all by-products in the lives of the people who have chosen to use this book in their daily affairs. Far from being a crutch, the Bible has allowed people to live their lives without crutches, by instilling the highest standards of morality, conduct and responsibility deep within their hearts.

Abraham Lincoln, a man whose influence in American history is unsurpassed, recognized that the Bible is not something to be considered an optional resource. To Lincoln it was an essential navigator, guiding us through each and every trial we face as we journey through life. In referring to this navigator he said, "The best gift God has given man…But for it we could not know right from wrong."

We have seen how many of our United States presidents, world-famous men of science and other great names of the past have spoken about the importance and influence of this one book. A few more quotes from important people of the past should help us better comprehend just how wide the scope of the Bible really is.

Daniel Webster, a great U.S. political leader and orator of the nineteenth century, once said, "If we abide by the principles taught by the Bible, our country will go on prospering." (43)

Timothy Dwight, a past President of Yale University, was keenly aware of the world around him. He once commented, "The Bible is a window in this prison world which we may look into eternity." (44)

Heinrich Heine, an influential German poet of the eighteenth century, called the Bible "The great medicine chest of humanity." (45)

Horace Greely was a U.S. editor and political leader. In addition to popularizing the saying, "Go West young man, go West," he understood how this idea was only possible in a land where real freedoms are protected. He also said:

> "It is impossible to mentally or socially enslave a Bible-reading people. The principles of the Bible are the groundwork of human freedom." (46)

A final reflection from Samuel Morse, the inventor of telegraph, follows:

> "The nearer I approach to the end of my pilgrimage, the clearer is the evidence of the divine origin of the Bible, the grandeur and sublimity of God's remedy for fallen man are more appreciated, and the future is illumined with hope and joy." (47)

Is reading the Bible a sign that one can't make it in this world alone? Clearly none of us can survive on our own without interpersonal contacts. Living in a vacuum or by ourselves on a deserted island has its way of shortening our lifespan drastically. Those who choose to consult with an unseen partner (and the Book that is all about Him) need not be ashamed or accused of leaning on a crutch. Rather, they have chosen a course where honesty, integrity and the highest standards of excellence promise to be their traveling companions as they journey through life.

Challenge 4 – It Has Been Rewritten Too Often To Be Trusted

So many people say, "How can you trust a book that was written over 2,000 years ago? It's so full of errors and discrepancies and has been rewritten and edited so often that only the gullible would rely on it." This is one of the greatest pieces of bad press ever hurled against the Bible. This belief is totally unfounded and just flat-out wrong. Let's examine the evidence.

How do you know that a person named George Washington ever really existed? Since he lived from 1732 to 1799, there can be no one alive today who personally knew him. This being the case, we are left with the only other option, and that is history. We know he existed because we can read all about him in numerous books. No one would ever say that Washington never existed, although only history can prove that he did. Many contend that 200 years ago is one thing but that 2,000 years ago is too far back to really rely on the validity of a book.

In order to judge just how reliable the biblical documents we have today are, we must put them through the same tests that historians place all ancient historical documents through. The principles of historiography are universally applied by scholars to determine the historical reliability of any document; the chief one is the bibliographical test.

The test is simple. Since we don't have the original manuscripts for any ancient writings, we must consider how reliable the copies we do have are in relation to how many of these copies we currently possess and the time interval between the original and extant copies.

The New Testament

If we were to compare the New Testament documents in this way, with other ancient historical works, a most amazing result would begin to emerge. Consider the following:

Caesar compiled his history of the Gallic Wars between 58 and 50 B.C. However, we only know of this event from nine or ten copies that date 900 years after he lived.

Josh McDowell tells us,

"Aristotle wrote his poetics around 343 B.C. and yet
the earliest copy we have is dated A.D. 1100, nearly
a 1,400-year gap, and only five manuscripts are in
existence." (48)

The history of Thucydides (460-400 B.C.) is available to us from
eight manuscripts that date from A.D. 900. That's a gap of almost
1,300 years. F. F. Bruce noted that the bibliographical evidence for the
history of Herodotus (480-425 B.C.) is similar to that of Thucydides,

"Yet no classical scholar would listen to an argument
that the authenticity of Herodotus or Thucydides is in
doubt because the earliest manuscripts of their works
which are of any use to us are over 1,300 years later
than the originals." (49)

When we consider the number of extant manuscripts of the New
Testament that are in existence today, the numbers are almost too
incredible to imagine. Scholars today possess over 4,000 ancient Greek
New Testament copies, another 8,000 manuscripts of the Latin and
at least 1,000 versions written in Syriac and other languages. That
totals 13,000 manuscript copies of the New Testament and all of them
essentially agree. The great New Testament authority Dr. F. J. A. Hort
stated that only about one word in a thousand is in sufficient question
to require a textual critic to discern the correct reading. (50) In many
of these cases we find that the scribe inverted a word order or copied a
letter wrong. The book that is second in manuscript authority to the
New Testament is *The Iliad*, which has 643 extant manuscripts.

Sir Frederic Kenyon, one of the greatest authorities of all time on
ancient manuscripts, stated,

"The interval then between the dates of original
composition and the earliest extant evidence becomes
so small as to be in fact negligible, and the last
foundation for any doubt that the Scriptures have come
down to us substantially as they were written has now
been removed. Both the authenticity and the general

77

integrity of the books of the New Testament may be regarded as finally established." (51)

Without a doubt the Bible has been established with greater certainty than any other ancient book ever penned. Imagine: over 13,000 ancient manuscripts are presently in existence. They were written in different languages, during different time periods, in different cultural settings and by many different people; yet all are alike.

The Old Testament

As we turn to the credibility of the Old Testament we once again shall enlist the aid of our friend the scientist to shed some light on the significance of the now-famous Dead Sea Scrolls. The discovery of these ancient scrolls, in the words of Gerald Lankester Harding, the British director of the Department of Antiquities in Amman Jordan, are "Perhaps the most sensational archaeological event of our time." (52) The *Encyclopedia Britannica* terms their recovery as follows: "Taken together, these manuscript finds are without precedent in the history of modern archaeology." (53) Just what is all this excitement about?

In 1947, a Bedouin shepherd boy, while hunting for a lost lamb on the north shore of the Dead Sea, stumbled upon some old scrolls of writing, which he thought were of little value. One of these scrolls were a 23-foot-long one, which contained the complete text of the Book of Isaiah in Hebrew. When experts began to examine this and other scrolls, they soon realized that they were quite old. In order to scientifically determine their age, the scrolls were flown to the United States, to the University of Chicago, in 1949.

Professor Willard F. Libby, at the Chicago Institute of Nuclear Physics, conducted a procedure that is now considered to be scientifically accurate beyond any doubt, called Carbon 14 dating.

Basically, scientists, with the use of Geiger-counters, can determine the rate of radioactive decay of Carbon 14. Since it takes 5,600 years for carbon to lose half of its original radioactivity, scientists can use this knowledge to extrapolate the age of any organic substance.

Both the Carbon 14 dating method and the incredibly detailed examination of papyrologists came up with the same astonishing conclusion: that the Isaiah manuscript was copied about 100 B.C.

When we compare this 2,000-year-old document with any present Bible, the significance of this discovery begins to come to light. First, both of these Isaiah texts have the exact same number of chapters: sixty-six. And second, when we compare each text, word for word, we find that they are virtually identical. There can now be no doubt that the Old Testament you hold in your hands today is identical to the ones used by Jesus and the other religious leaders of 2,000 years ago.

Prior to the discovery of the Dead Sea Scrolls, the earliest Hebrew complete manuscript (and Hebrew was the original language in which the Old Testament was written) we had was from A.D. 900. That brings us 1,000 years closer to the original documents in one fell swoop. Needless to say, the excitement generated from this find sparked an unprecedented exploration of desert caves and ancient ruins around the Dead Sea.

So far to date, over 400 ancient manuscripts have been uncovered, 100 being biblical. Of the thirty-nine different books of the Old Testament, only one book has not been found, the Book of Esther. They all date from around 200 B.C. to A.D. 100.

Together these findings should forever silence the critics who contend that the Bible we have today has been rewritten so often as to be of little trustworthiness. The scholars who have thoroughly investigated this stunning discovery have told us that the few variations that do exist between the Dead Sea Scrolls and our oldest Hebrew manuscripts from A.D. 900 are so small as to be negligible in altering the meaning of any of the text.

Can we trust the Bible we have today? I dare say that if we don't, we must also throw out all the other ancient works of history and consider them unreliable. Both historians and scientists alike have left us with no other alternative but to acknowledge that the Bible we have in our possession is virtually the same as that which the scribes of 2,000 years ago so meticulously copied.

Challenge 5—It's Dull

If a visitor from another planet were to beam down right in the middle of the stands of an NFL football game, I wonder what he would think. Seeing twenty-two men running up and down a 100-yard field in ferocious pursuit of an oblong ball, to the deafening roar of 60,000 screaming fans, for three hours, just might cause our visitor to wonder what in the world is going on. If we then went on to explain to him that these 60,000 fans were having a great, exciting time, we probably would totally confound our alien guest.

While we know that "beauty is in the eye of the beholder," the concept of what makes something exciting or dull equally depends on who we ask and the perspective we view the situation from. A few of the more popular criticisms and misconceptions that many people use to explain why they feel the Bible is a "big dull book" on the surface seem to have some merit.

Biblical opponents claim that there are endless lists of genealogies of men who in many cases have names that are impossible to pronounce. Others contend that there are too many Thee's, Thou's and whosoevers, that it's difficult to read and understand. Another criticism is that there is too much repetition of phrases for the fast-paced readers of today. Finally, many believe that it is just too darn big a book to read.

Our little foreign friend from the football game would probably, if presented with a new Bible, agree with the above comments. But if he would just take the time to begin reading the Bible, armed with a little background information, and allow his negative preconceived notions to stand on the sidelines for a while, he might begin to see something wonderful emerge.

Granted, Thee's, Thou's and whosoevers are a bit archaic. They tend to make reading the Bible an arduous task for many new readers. This is because the most famous Bible translation in America, the *King James Version*, was written in 1611, in Elizabethan English. While 1611 English was quite natural to the ear of a 1611 citizen, it isn't today. Fortunately for us, there are many contemporary translations that are quite excellent, *The New American Standard Bible* and the *New International Version* of the Bible are two current examples. These are written in Modern English and are quite easy and enjoyable to read. The Thee's and Thou's are gone and so is one major stumbling block to those who are scared to open this precious book.

It is also true that 750,000 words for one book is certainly a lot of reading for an individual. Part of the uniqueness of the Bible is that while it is one book, it consists in reality of sixty-six books, thirty-nine in the Old Testament and twenty-seven in the New Testament.

Each of these sixty-six books is an integral part of the entire biblical narrative. Yet each book can also be read alone as a single unit and amazingly tell a wonderful story all on its own. If we approach the Scriptures in this way, we now no longer have quite so imposing a book to deal with.

The Bible is like a giant tapestry. Each of its books acts as a thread; together they give us the fullness of the beauty and grandeur of God's Word. Reading it all or one book at a time, the reader can rest assured that wisdom, excitement and fascinating reading lie within his grasp.

The Key to good public speaking is the ability to keep listeners interested and also to have them remember the message. One very effective way to accomplish this is through the skillful repetition of the subject matter, from different angles and stories. That is exactly what the Bible sets out to do.

Important themes, such as God's love, mercy and judgments, are repeated over and over throughout the entire Bible, but they are colorfully presented by different writers through different people, situations and places. In this way the reader begins to have the meat of the Word become more and more a part of his memory.

The seemingly endless genealogies also play an important role. They challenge our minds to ponder the great expanses of history the Bible covers. They also help us to understand the linkages from one period to another and piece together ancient history.

The Reading Experience Of A Lifetime

With these few helpful hints under our belts, let's sit back and relax as we travel into the fabulous world of the Bible. There is more action, adventure, romance, intrigue, wisdom, life and inspiration in this one volume than in any other book ever written. It is a breathtaking, panoramic saga of kings, empires and dynasties, vividly described in the rich, full texture of an ancient world setting. Great wealth and splendor are continuously contrasted with the everyday life and affairs of the common man.

The forty-plus authors, although spanning a period of 1,500 years, remarkably managed to connect all sixty-six books into a thrilling tale of man and his quest for meaning. Layer upon layer of man's intensely complex personality and emotions are laid bare before us, as the reader is given the most in-depth exploration into the very essence of our human nature.

Stories that many of us have heard about all of our lives, but perhaps have never read, provide the backdrop for the examination of our human condition. Adam and Eve, Cain and Abel, Noah's ark, Samson and Delilah, the tower of Babel, David and Goliath, the Ten Commandments, Jonah and the whale, Moses and the parting of the Red Sea, Daniel and the lion's den, the three wise men, Jesus born in a manger, the crucifixion of Jesus and His coming back to life, and many more, become alive to us as we begin to explore our Bibles.

Most books present their readers with a theme, some story information, perhaps entertainment, and a conclusion. These books are read, but after a while fade into our distant memories. But the Bible is not called the "Book of books" for nothing. It is totally multidimensional in its scope. It's a mirror. As we read it, we constantly see ourselves reflected in the lives of the biblical characters. It's a treasure hunt. As we travel through its pages, we are guaranteed to find nuggets of wisdom of incomparable value. Proverbs 3:13-15 declares:

> *How blessed is the man who finds wisdom, and the man who gains understanding. For its profit is better than the profit of silver, and its gain than fine gold. She is more precious than jewels; and nothing you desire compares with her.*

The Bible is history. As we have already seen, the Bible is a first-rate history book that promises to send any history buff into a state of sheer ecstasy. The Bible is full of poetry. The Book of Psalms is world-renowned for its literary style and excellence of composition. It's philosophy. The Holy Scriptures have more to say about human nature and what life is all about than Plato, Socrates, Aristotle, Confucius and Freud combined. It's science. Once again not only does the Bible talk authoritatively on many areas in the scientific realm, but it has been the indispensable mentor of many of the greatest scientific men of all time.

It's inspirational. Jesus' teachings on the Sermon on the Mount, the Psalms, the Ten Commandments and the continuous love of God for mankind have down through the centuries been the pillars on which millions have anchored their faith. No Book can generate more comfort, encouragement and purpose for living than the Bible. So many great masterpieces of art, literature, music and film have been created by people touched with the message of God that our world would be deprived of much of its very heart and soul if it were deprived of this one book.

Its message is powerful. Hebrews 4:12 boldly proclaims:

> *For the word of God is living and active and sharper than any two-edged sword, and piercing as far as the division of soul and spirit, of both joints and marrow, and able to judge the thoughts and intentions of the heart.*

Winkie Pratney rightly stated:

> "You know, many of the Eastern thought forms use Scripture. That's because the book is so powerful— you can't ignore it. If you don't use it, you can't capture people's hearts. God has built life into His Word, and all of the strong cults rip it off—steal bites out of the Bible and use it...Just the fact that pieces taken out of context are powerful enough to draw men's hearts should tell you what the whole Word, used under the inspiration of the Holy Spirit can do." (54)

Finally, the Bible is ultra-controversial. No book has caused more people to be burned at the stake, brought before firing squads, sent to prison, beheaded, stoned, sawn in two, subjected to scourgings, mocked and made a spectacle of than the Bible. It's hard to believe how one "dull old book" can rile people up to such states of hatred and murder.

My friends, the genius behind this collection of sixty-six books is without rival on planet Earth. Imagine: all of the above themes, and the chance to find peace, joy and meaning in our lives, are all wrapped up in one volume. You just may find yourself embarking on a scenic tour into a world you never dreamed could exist.

In Summary

This chapter has presented five challenges in an attempt to expose, once and for all, some of the myths and bad press the Bible has had to face down through the centuries. Attacks have been waged against it from every area and discipline imaginable; but the Bible's resiliency and ability to defend its contents speak for themselves. Any book that has been on the best-seller list for 2,000 years (that's over 100,000 weeks) must have something going for it. It's kind of like chicken soup. It can't hurt you, but it just might have the right remedy you need to bring healing and true meaning into your life.

Chapter 7
The Bible Said It First

If you have ever picked up a book of famous quotations, several things immediately begin to manifest themselves. First, you instantly recognize many old sayings, proverbs and maxims you have heard over and over again since your youth. Second, the distilled wisdom from famous person after famous person is quoted on every subject under the sun. Finally, you notice that many of the statements presented are quite true.

Without perhaps realizing it, a wealth of profoundly influential yet simple statements that are well known to all of us found their origination in the Bible. Even without reading the Bible, your life has been molded by its pages far more than you might think. Listed below are nine examples from literally hundreds of simple verses found in the Holy Scriptures that, taken as a whole, could revolutionize your life if put into practice. They have been time-tested for 2,000 years and still ring true in our ears today.

Verse 1—(Acts 20:35). "It is more blessed to give than to receive."
In 1872 a young man of thirty-three became a millionaire. By 1882, just ten years later, this same individual, at the still young age of forty-three, was in control of the largest business in the world. By the time 1892 rolled around, just twenty years after that first million was made, John D. Rockefeller had parlayed that small fortune into a cool billion dollars. At age fifty-three, John D. became the only billionaire in the world.

Few men have been as obsessed as John D. Rockefeller was in making money. He was possessed by a driving force that might cause us to redefine "workaholic." Coupled with this unquenchable desire to make money was a lack of consideration for others. In fact he hurled many a helpless competitor into bankruptcy. He was so hated that these same now penniless individuals hanged him in effigy in the oil fields of Pennsylvania.

Unfortunately for John D., by the time he reached fifty-three he could little enjoy his weekly income of one million dollars. He had contracted a condition called alopecia. Not only did he lose the hair off his head, but he lost most of the hair off his eyelashes and eyebrows. In addition, his digestion became so bad that he could only eat crackers and milk.

He looked like death warmed over. It was the general consensus that he wouldn't see his fifty-fourth birthday. In fact, the newspapers had already written his obituary and expected to use it any day. His health was gone, his sleep had fled him, and the only thing he had left to him was his haunting memories of a life of misery.

With death knocking at the door, John D. Rockefeller, suddenly, in a moment of insight, began to contemplate a concept spoken of by Jesus Christ: "It is more blessed to give than to receive." From that point on his entire outlook on life radically changed. Instead of hoarding his great wealth, he began to give it away as fast as he had made it. Hospitals, universities and millions of less fortunate people were blessed by one man's generosity, unparalleled in the history of humanity. When all was said and done his philanthropies totaled some $500 million.

Just as there are certain physical laws that govern our universe, there are also God's eternal laws that dictate our emotional well-being. Perhaps without knowing the source, John D. Rockefeller accepted the challenge of Acts 20:35 and started to put into practice the blessed act of giving. Almost immediately his sleep returned to him. He began to eat normally and life finally started to be enjoyable. In return for his generosity he received the gift of life, to the tune of an extra forty-five years of living, till the ripe old age of ninety-eight.

Not only did the greatest philanthropist of all time discover that it is indeed more blessed to give than to receive, but that in reality when you give, you receive also. Forty-five years more life, and the admiration of the entire world, were credited to the account of John D. Rockefeller the moment he began to share his wealth.

Verse 2—(Genesis 1:1). "In the beginning God created the heavens and the earth."

In The winter of 1968, a historic event took place that sent excitement throughout the entire world as few events had ever done before. The spaceship Apollo 8 made the first voyage from our planet to the moon. Commander Frank Borman, Jim Lovell and Bill Anders became the first men to orbit the moon. The complete fascination of our globe was captured by this mission. It was estimated that over one billion people would be watching them. These three men were granted the extraordinary privilege of being the first humans to view the moon from a window away.

Early in the morning of December 21, 1968, the blastoff took place from Cape Kennedy with flawless perfection. Commander Borman was well aware of the significance of this first historic flight, the mammoth audience that would have their eyes riveted to their T.V. sets, and the incredible opportunity the Apollo 8 crew had to do something special. Borman had thought long and hard on what his crew might prepare to say to a world that would be eagerly watching them. Finally a suggestion was made to read the creation story. The rest is history. While orbiting the moon, with the earth behind them and the entire universe before them, over one billion people began to hear the opening ten verses from Genesis.

I can imagine the excitement, the drama and the impact that must have been generated as the following words came into the ears of those firsthand hearers from almost 250,000 miles away: "In the beginning God created the heavens and the earth." As the rest of the verses were read one could not help but stand in awe at this remarkable technological accomplishment, of man and nature rendezvousing in a never-before-journeyed-to corridor of our galaxy. It is only fitting that the creation story was read on man's first flight to the moon. God's Word has now not only been circulated throughout this world but to other worlds as well.

Again, whenever the Bible is read, controversy is bound to follow. This time, however, when all the returns were in, the Bible won by a landslide. In the words of Frank Borman: "One woman in particular began a campaign to prohibit astronauts from expressing their views in this way. She did have a certain following, because we received 34 letters of complaint. But it is interesting that there were almost 100,000 other letters from people who found the Genesis reading very meaningful indeed." (55) If a simple verse can generate such excitement, imagine what the entire Bible can do.

Verse 3—(Mark 8:36). "For what does it profit a man to gain the whole world, and forfeit his soul?"

Just how much are you worth? If they were to add up all of their weekly paychecks, by year end most people would find that they had earned anywhere from $10,000 to $100,000. The average wage earner would probably say that he is worth approximately $30,000 to $60,000 a year. That's one way of looking at how much you are worth.

Many people, when they take inventory of their financial position, realize that, if they were to die, their spouse would be the beneficiary of their life insurance policy proceeds. With the advent of "term insurance," many people now have $100,000 in coverage. Viewing it from this angle, your worth would now carry a price tag of $100,000.

A chemist one day investigated how much all the different substances that make up our body are worth. Distilling us down into the very elements we are composed of, he found that, if we sold all of them in the open market, each one of us would be worth about $5 million.

But, may I challenge you to consider that you are worth far more than even $5 million. In fact most of us are multibillionaires today, and don't even know it. Before you say that your bank account would certainly indicate otherwise, think about the following: Would you be willing to accept a tax-free gift of, say, $1 billion? The only stipulation is that in return for this gift you would have to forfeit your eyesight.

With one billion dollars you could do everything you ever dreamed possible, only you would have to do it in complete, eternal darkness. Most people, I believe, would refuse to make this deal, thus acknowledging how rich they really are.

But our often-quoted Scripture verse places your worth still much higher than this. If you all of a sudden were to lose one of your legs, you would still be you. If you lost both legs your name wouldn't change. Even if you were to lose both legs and both arms, your very essence wouldn't change one bit. This is because your personality, your thoughts, your emotions and your will are all intangible and invisible, yet vital to describing who you really are. Your external frame just provides a covering for the real you. And at the very core of who you are lies what the Bible refers to as your soul—your very essence.

God's Word says, "For what does it profit a man to gain the whole world, and forfeit his soul?" Clearly the Bible realizes that your soul is worth more than the entire world. Think about it. You could own the entire planet Earth, but if you die and your soul becomes no more, or, as the Bible states, becomes eternally separated from God, where would you be?

Just how much are you worth? Your value is infinite. Take a little time to ponder just how valuable you really are. You might begin to place your priorities in life in a slightly different order.

Verse 4—(Ecclesiastes 1:9). "There is nothing new under the sun."
We are living in a technological renaissance where nothing now seems impossible, thanks to man's genius in the area of science. Evidence of this explosion of knowledge and innovation runs rampant throughout the world. We have already landed men on the moon. Transplants of organs such as the heart and kidney are now commonplace. Computers can now solve in seconds problems that would have taken a man years to do in the past.

But all of this is just the fringe of a new era of science fiction becoming science fact. Within the next twenty years man may find a cure for cancer, replace skilled laborers with robots, and even destroy his entire world with several thousand thermal nuclear devices if he is not careful. For the past 5,000 years mankind has been traveling on a technological exponential curve, with no end in sight. From skyscrapers to calculators, from micro-surgery to telecommunications, man has truly outdone himself.

I will admit that outwardly there is definitely plenty that is new, in our present age, under the sun. On the inside, however, there really isn't anything new under the sun. Over the same 5,000 years, man's inner being, his so-called human nature—what curve has it taken? Unfortunately this curve has been at best flat and probably declining.

Has man been able to see any corresponding advances in his morality? Sadly, there has been no advance and "nothing new" in his makeup. As a moral creature mankind, as history will bear out, has never changed for the better; if anything it has gotten worse. Just examine a tiny fraction of the evidence over the last 150 years:

- In 1857 the United States Supreme Court ruled that blacks were to be considered property. They were also to have no civil rights at all.
- Up until 1920 and the passing of the Nineteenth Amendment to the United States Constitution, women in the U.S.A. couldn't vote in most of our states.
- During Word War II (1939-1945), over 6 million Jews were exterminated by Adolf Hitler and Nazi Germany.
- Before 1947 and Jackie Robinson, no blacks were allowed to play major-league baseball.
- Today millions of people in Africa literally are dying of hunger while the United States has millions of tons of wheat in silos around our country.
- Yearly over 50 million abortions, worldwide, are performed.

Man's nature hasn't changed, nor has his outlook on life. As you read the following discourse from Ecclesiastes, you can sense the great state of restlessness that humankind is continually undergoing:

> *"Vanity of vanities," says the Preacher, "vanity of vanities. All is vanity." What advantage does man have in all his work which he does under the sun? A generation goes and a generation comes, but the earth remains forever. Also, the sun rises and the sun sets; and hastening to its place it rises there again. Blowing toward the south, then turning toward the north, the wind continues swirling along; and on its circular courses the wind returns. All the rivers flow into the sea, yet the sea is not full. To the place where the rivers flow, there they flow again. All things are wearisome; man is not able to tell it. The eye is not satisfied with*

seeing, nor is the ear filled with hearing. That which has been is that which will be, and that which has been done is that which will be done. So, there is nothing new under the sun.

Ecclesiastes 1:2-9

Once again, the Bible has been able to accurately depict the state of mankind 2,000 years into the future.

Verse 5—(Romans 12:19). "VENGEANCE IS MINE."

These three words pack one of the most important messages you may ever hear. This often-quoted Bible passage is only a portion of Romans 12:19. The full verse reads,

Never take your own revenge, beloved, but leave room for the wrath of God, for it is written, "VENEANCE IS MINE, I WILL REPAY, SAYS THE LORD."

In an earlier chapter we discussed how our minds play an important part in the overall health of our bodies. The whole field of psychosomatic illness became a hard reality to us as we touched upon how faulty emotions can wreak havoc with just about every part of our bodies.

Here we come to another one of God's eternal laws. This law of negative emotions states that if we continue to harbor thoughts of anger, hatred and bitterness toward others, over time the decay and destruction of our bodies is certain.

In our present environment, where so much of the vitality of life depends upon the things we can see and touch, it is utterly remarkable how in actuality the invisible forces in our universe dominate every avenue of our existence.

The air we breathe is essential for living. Without it we would die in a matter of minutes; yet it is invisible. The force that holds our planet Earth in orbit around the sun, gravity, again cannot be seen with our eyes. Whenever we turn on a light, radio, T.V. or one of the host of modern appliances in our homes, the energy source that makes them all work, electricity, is invisible to us.

The chair you are sitting on is made up of countless trillions of atoms, so tiny that nobody can see them. According to Kenneth Taylor,

> "Since it is true that atoms are mostly empty space dotted occasionally by weightless electrons with great distance between, it is also true that the chair you are sitting on is mostly nothingness, held together by the force of whirling electrons moving so rapidly that they cannot be crushed. No wonder the Bible says that the things that appear are made of things not seen." (56)

Yes, even our thoughts are invisible and weightless. How we use them, however, holds the keys to our emotional well being and ultimately our health. If we allow ourselves to hold bitter feelings toward others, hoping that we can somehow take revenge on them or that they get what they deserve, we are setting into motion an elaborate self-destruct mechanism.

Our thoughts either carry positive or negative energy. Bitterness is a negatively charged thought that is transmitted, by the brain, throughout the entire body, reaching trillions of cells in a matter of seconds. This great cell disrupter over days, months and years is electrocuting, in a sense, all of our bodily systems. Not only that, if we are not careful, this negatively charged energy will literally blast holes in our stomachs, colon and intestines, bring about massive ruptures in our arteries and in many cases cause our hearts to beat no more.

God knew all of this and wisely admonished us to allow Him to handle the whole vengeance question. When we turn this burden over to Him, our load becomes much lighter. But the Bible goes a step further and gives us a third eternal law. The first law we saw earlier is the law of giving. The second is the law of negative emotions. The third can be summed up best by another verse, well familiar to us all: "YOU SHALL LOVE YOUR NEIGHBOR AS YOURSELF" (Galatians 5:14).

If we allowed this timeless advice to govern our lives, we would see such a surge of positive energy pulsating throughout our bodies that there would be little room left to house the negative thoughts we so often dwell upon.

Verse 6—(Matthew 26:41). "The spirit is willing, but the flesh is weak."

Procrastination seems to be a preoccupation as well as a national pastime for most Americans. So often we find that we set our minds on doing something, yet our bodies never seem to follow along. Our dreams never seem to become realities. Our resolutions have to be renewed every New Year's Day. Even the commitments we make are not often kept. Our good intentions are in constant battle with a force that many times is so overpowering that we fall helpless to its advances.

It's as if each of us is involved in a boxing match, but this time our opponent is ourselves. In one corner we have our spirit or our will. In the other corner we have the challenger, our flesh or emotions. Unfortunately for our combatants there are no rest periods between rounds, and the rounds never seem to end.

Our minds are engaged in a great civil war where our spirit and flesh are constantly vying for supremacy. This confrontation of will and emotions has provided our nation's psychiatrists and psychologists with an endless stream of battle-scarred and weary individuals. Self-help books abound everywhere, each claiming to be the solution to our problems.

The Bible, however, has a remarkable way of distilling many a complex problem into one short sentence. Not only that, but it has a way of not wasting any words. In just nine short words, the Bible states the universal dilemma and condition of mankind.

In "the spirit is willing, but the flesh is weak," we see several pieces of the puzzle that interlock perfectly in describing why we are the way we are. First we see that man is endowed with a spirit. Our drives, desires, ambitions and character are all parts of our spirit nature. All of these facets of our makeup are controlled to a large extent by and through our wills.

The will acts like the commander-in-chief of our little band of characteristics, giving them their marching orders. Often our battle plans for our lives are well mapped out. A carefully plotted course and destination all seem well within reach. However, right in the middle of our nine-word "statement of condition" lies the pivotal word, "but." As with so many things in life there always seems to be a "but."

"But the flesh is weak." The flesh represents our emotional center, and here is where the real battle is fought. So often this center is like a huge mine field, where every turn seems to be loaded with powerful booby traps. These can destroy our well laid plans quite quickly if we are not trained properly to avoid them.

It is here that the Holy Scriptures provide us with tremendous insight into why we have such an uphill battle in life. For we read, "the flesh is weak." There is something in our human nature that is flawed and weak. And no matter how hard we try, we never seem to gain the freedom we so desperately need to live our lives to the fulfillment of the dreams we have.

The Bible gives this flaw a name: "sin." We discussed earlier how when Adam disobeyed God by eating the forbidden fruit, he fell into sin, broke fellowship with God, and passed this flaw on to everyone who ever lived after him.

Ponder the above scenario and see how it so perfectly depicts the state of man today. For most of us, the great potential we all possess never really gets off the ground. Our flesh so often wins the battle over the spirit. It's time to take inventory. For many, peace of mind, joy and true meaning in life never seem to be found. Instead they find, when they look back on their lives in old age, only memories of what could have been. When they look forward, they see only a future fast approaching its terminal point. Little if any meaning has been found.

Such a person, who was of supreme importance to him or herself, history will record just as a statistical blip in time. As grim as this may appear we shall vividly display a different potential outlook in the final two chapters of this book. The Bible offers us an alternative of great hope, and freedom from the bondage we so often find ourselves in.

Verse 7—(Deuteronomy 5:17). "You shall not murder."

In one of the greatest Hollywood epics of all time, the silver screen vividly portrays Charlton Heston being given the two tablets of stone on which were written, by the finger of God, the Ten Commandments. The "Ten Commandments," however, represent far more than a four-star motion picture blockbuster. They represent the ten moral laws given by God to Moses on Mount Sinai when the Israelites were in the desert.

Their importance to Christians, Jews and Moslems throughout the world cannot be underestimated. These ten statements of behavior form the core of ethics for 1.5 billion people. These ten basic laws, found in the Holy Scriptures, also form the basic code of behavior by which the rest of the world intrinsically lives.

As the lightning flashes through the heavens, Charlton Heston, as Moses, is treated to a magnificent display of holy engraving as God permanently etches in stone these monumental words:

> *You shall not murder. You shall not commit adultery. You shall not steal. You shall not bear false witness against your neighbor. You shall not covet your neighbor's wife, and you shall not desire your neighbor's house...*
> Deuteronomy 5:17-21

This portion of the Decalogue, written 3,500 years ago, forms the basic tenets on which our legal system is based. It is often contended that everybody knows that these commandments should be obeyed. When we break one of them, our consciences clearly let us know about it. On the surface, this statement seems quite valid. But if it were not for these ancient guidelines, our sense of right and wrong, our morality, and our legal system would have turned out quite differently.

Those of us who have raised children know that constantly hammering home these principles is crucial to bringing up children. The beauty and innocence of our precious tiny babies quickly fade as they reach toddlerhood. By the time your little angel has reached three years old, examine how many times you have had to say: "No," "Don't do that," "That's wrong," "Stop that," and a host of other words of warning.

A little baby has no real sense of right or wrong. How babies view things, interact with people and react to situations are to a great extent the product of what we teach them. If we never said no or administered appropriate punishments in these critical first years of life, the little monsters we turn out would be a nightmare too horrifying to contemplate. They have fortunately had the wisdom and knowledge of right and wrong taught to them by parents who in turn have had the insights of the Bible passed down to them through countless generations before them.

If the only thing the Bible ever gave to mankind was these wonderful moral teachings to live by, that alone would make this one book of unquestionable value. But, as we have seen, this is just one of many facets possessed by a book that, the more you examine it, the more it examines you.

Verse 8—(I Timothy 6:10 KJV). "For the love of money is the root of all evil."

Money, this medium of exchange, is crucial to almost every area of our lives. Without it, we can't buy food, clothes, shelter and a host of other essentials to everyday life. Without a doubt it is the number-one yardstick in the world by which success is measured. The more you have of it, the more success society attributes to you. It is also critical to all of the status symbols we strive to obtain.

The Big house, fancy car, mink coat, pleasure boat and country club membership all depend on our possessing a large sum of greenbacks. Now there is absolutely nothing wrong with having these status symbols or a large bank account. Even the Bible, which many people feel condemns individuals who have a lot of money, offers no condemnation to the accumulation of wealth. In fact many of the greatest and most beloved biblical characters were quite wealthy. Men such as Abraham, King David, Job and Solomon would all be considered multimillionaires today.

The crucial question, however, is: Do you possess your money, or does your money possess you? As we saw earlier, John D. Rockefeller was clearly obsessed and possessed by his own wealth. His love of money caused all sorts of evil to befall him.

In an effort to own many of the status symbols mentioned above, millions of Americans have sacrificed their home lives by working inordinate hours to the great neglect of their families. Many more have traded in their health in return for these perishable commodities, by worrying and concentrating all their energies and waking hours on how to obtain them. Finally, great numbers of Americans who don't have much money still have managed to buy what they want through the plastic medium of VISA and Master Card. But in the end they have buried themselves in debt and in some cases bankruptcy.

When you come right down to it, the things that really matter in life and form the real barometer for our own happiness don't depend on money. Friendships, a family, a good name, and peace of mind are all well within the reach of all of us.

A simple test should suffice to drive home the reality of this statement. Money is basically good for supplying us with material things. As these things grow old, wear out and become used up, examine the memories you have of them. They are not lasting and only create an unquenchable desire to replace them or have more of them.

On the other hand, when we examine our memories of good friends, our children and our honor and reputation, a gentle warmth and good feeling seem to always accompany them; and it lasts. Think about it. Are you in control of your money or has your money taken control over you? If the latter appears to be the case, be prepared, for evil awaits you.

Verse 9—(Psalm 53:1). "The fool has said in his heart, 'There is no God.'"

With the advent of Charles Darwin, the belief in a divine Creator was given a severe blow. Science today, to a large extent, has dismissed the idea. There are people in our own government who are even considering taking "In God We Trust" off our coins and bills, thus tacitly casting their vote against God also.

The great Albert Einstein, who many believe was the greatest scientist who ever lived, concluded that our universe was so orderly, rational and logical that it demanded a Creator or God. To Einstein, to think that random, blind chance was the cause of the creation of our universe was an insult to his intelligence. Einstein believed that the most amazing thing about our universe was not that we couldn't comprehend all of it, but that we could in fact comprehend a tiny portion of it.

Dr. Gustaf Stromberg, staff astronomer of Mount Wilson observatory, concluded,

"I believe that behind the physical world we see with our eyes and study in our telescopes and microscopes, and measure with our instruments of various kinds is another, more fundamental, realm which cannot be described in physical terms. In this nonphysical realm lies the ultimate origin of all things, of energy, matter, organization and life and consciousness." (57)

Frank Borman, our astronaut from verse 2, said:

"The more we learn about the wonders of our universe, the more clearly we are going to perceive the hand of God." (58)

The agnostic and the atheist who live their lives without a belief in a divine Creator must indeed lead a lonely life. By definition they must believe that they have no soul and no immortality. Since they came into existence by chance, and not divine design, any meaning they find in life is but a by-product of random occurrences. Even the great mysteries of our universe that cause us to ponder just who we are and why we are here are a closed corridor of thought to those who place God as something that exists only in one's imagination.

The struggle of life for all of us, without the existence of a rational creative force in the background, makes our journey here on earth a mere exercise in futility. The only reality we all can count on is physical death. For the atheist, he will die, sadly without ever knowing why he was born in the first place.

Composite Wisdom

Strip away the historical nature of the Bible, its scientific validity, its tremendous inspirational qualities and its incredible indestructibility, and what you have left is pure wisdom. For over 2,000 years, man has been able to put to the test, through a myriad of personal experiences, the concepts taught in this age-old book.

The inevitable conclusion has been the same for countless generations: Our emotional well-being is directly tied to how closely we allow these pages of wisdom to penetrate and permeate our minds. The Bible indeed said it first when it comes to how to maintain a healthy mind and body; and nobody has been able to improve upon its timeless advice since.

Chapter 8
Will The Real Moon Please Stand Up?

If I were to say the word "moon" to you, what would be the first thought that comes to your mind? Chances are it would either be the celestial body or Reverend Sun Myung Moon. Between the two of them there exists one thing in common: both have been the object of worship. Down through the centuries, and especially in ancient times, the moon has often been worshipped as if it were a god. The Greeks, Romans and Egyptians each had their own moon gods, to whom they paid homage. Sacrifices were made to these gods and an elaborate system of rituals surrounded many ancient moon worship ceremonies. The mystery and magnificence of our closest heavenly body somehow had a magical and enchanting quality all its own that literally brought people to their knees in admiration.

Back in 1920 a new moon arose with an equally alluring mystique. His rise to fame and power as the head of the Unification Church made him the subject of countless news stories, television specials and daily conversation during the 1970's. Thousands of young Americans became followers of a man who once said, "I will conquer and subjugate the world." Moon also went on to add, "I am your brain." (59)

It was quite common, especially during the 1970's, to see these followers or "Moonies" selling flowers and candles on the streets of our American cities. The Moonies have sadly abandoned their families, material possessions, and lives to the "movement." They have been psychologically conditioned to bow down to this self-proclaimed messiah. Moon has been able to make his followers believe that he is a "Lord of the Second Advent" and a key player in the movement for world salvation.

Credentials

In order for someone or something to be worthy of worship, credentials of the highest order must not only be displayed but earned. What credentials do each of our moons have to offer us?

A full moon on a clear night has a way of causing our minds to stop for a moment and stare with awe and admiration at one of the most spectacular sights in our universe. Our planet has the privilege of having the most obedient traveling companion imaginable. Since its creation, this one satellite has stood by us through good and bad times, never leaving our side.

By its very nature the moon also is a very gentle and kind neighbor. By maintaining an average distance to us of 238,857 miles, it allows our ocean tides to calmly ebb and flow twice a day. If the moon ever decided to come a little closer to us, say 200,000 miles, tides of thirty-five to fifty feet would inundate (twice a day) a large part of the surface of our earth.

Beautiful, obedient and friendly, that's our neighbor the moon. But is it worthy of our worship? If you believe that our moon is the chance product of galactic evolution or a cataclysmic explosion or even cosmic condensation, then you would be quite foolish to put your trust in a dead ball of inanimate matter.

To those of us who hold that God created the universe, we also would be on dangerous grounds to put our faith in a celestial body. Deuteronomy 4:19 says,

> *And beware, lest you lift up your eyes to heaven and see the sun and the moon and the stars, all the host of heaven, and be drawn away and worship them and serve them, those which the LORD your God has allotted to all peoples under the whole heaven.*

What about the Reverend Moon? Wherever he has gone he has produced bondage, not freedom. His teachings and techniques have stripped away minds, not illuminated them. Finally, he is no savior, but a messenger of Satan in disguise.

While neither moon is deserving of our devotion, both are in fact symbols that represent two quite divergent views of the world we live in. One view has the potential to lead us to a higher plane of existence, while the other promises us a pathway to doom and destruction. Both moons are in a sense guiding lights. One will illuminate a brilliant world of life. The other will cast its shadow on a gloomy world of death. Let's go on to the pathways.

Nature – The Pathway Of Light

> *Then God said, "Let there be light;" and there was light.*
> *And God saw that the light was good; and God separated*
> *the light from the darkness. And God called the light day,*
> *and the darkness He called night. And there was evening*
> *and there was morning, one day.*
> Genesis 1:3-5

We live in a world of opposites. Concepts such as light and darkness, night and day, up and down and love and hate give us anchor points by which to measure our lives. One other set of opposites, "positive and negative," dictates the quality of life we all experience. We normally desire positive feelings, while striving to avoid the negative ones.

If God were to look for an ambassador to represent Himself to all the people of our planet, He would do well to choose creation itself to represent Himself, the Creator. Our natural world amply displays the creative genius, wondrous beauty and careful design of this master "Architect."

Not only that, but one of the most positive forces in our world today is our relationship with our natural environment. A brilliant sunset, a rainbow, a starry night and a rolling brook provide us with two important aspects of our existence.

First, they present us with glimpses into just how beautiful our planet Earth really can be. Psalm 19:1 eloquently states the second aspect: "The heavens are telling of the glory of God; and their expanse is declaring the work of His hands." Could chance have created the magnificence we are about to touch upon? Or could there just be a purpose and a gracious "Provider" behind it all?

The Redwoods

Take a tiny seed, put it in the ground, give it lots of water and sunshine and what do you get? Perhaps a watermelon, a tulip, or maybe a redwood tree. Before our redwood can be born its seed must sacrifice itself through death. Just what is a redwood tree? It can best be described below in the following tree biographical profile:

        1 seed
      300 feet tall
    6,000 tons heavy
    4,000 years old

Two hundred generations of human beings have come and gone since this single seed was buried in the ground. If you have ever visited these titanic timbers in Northern California, they would be guaranteed to leave you breathless. Our government was impressed enough with their awesome stature and beauty to declare them national monuments.

Man, with all his genius, can at best through good, clean living and modern medicine guarantee himself 70 to 100 years of life. Our redwood friends, with no education and no apparent wisdom, have somehow managed to thrive and grow century after century. By chance or by design, if the redwoods could speak, they just might have a fabulous tale to tell.

Niagara Falls

Known throughout our country as a popular tourist center, Niagara falls is a symbol of power, beauty and mystery. "Powerful" is a fitting word to describe the enormous volume of water that passes over the falls. Millions of gallons of water every minute, producing an awesome cloud of vapor, roar pass the awestruck eyes of the beholder.

Beauty is apparent to everyone who has had the privilege of getting an actual firsthand viewing of this spectacular show of flow, form and foam. Mystery and contemplation are two things that remain with us long after we have departed from the presence of the falls. I myself have often wondered, "Just how long has this great outpouring of water been cascading down? Is it centuries, millennia or even longer? Could the flow have started as a trickle, or as the flood we now see? Will the water ever stop flowing?"

Finally, I have long asked myself, "What kind of force could have created such a spectacular sight and powerful testimony of the magnificence of nature?" Niagara Falls has the handiwork of God amply written all over it. They wonderfully parallel the nature of God: power, beauty, mystery and an existence that seems to have no beginning or ending.

Water

This ideal liquid is unsurpassed in its functionality and its universality. Without this miracle substance our lives would soon cease to exist in a matter of days. Our bodies require this chemical compound for 1,001 processes. No wonder it has been called the "universal solvent." Man, despite his genius in the chemical labs around the world, has still not been able to produce a substance as unique and beneficial as this naturally occurring one.

Water is a chemical composition of hydrogen and oxygen. It consists of two atoms of hydrogen to every one of oxygen. Water is an amazing substance that naturally exists in all three states of matter: gas, liquid and solid. Ice, snow, rain, hail and sleet are some of the many meteorological forms it can assume. Hydrogen and oxygen, two distinct and very different elements, somehow have learned to combine to form a colorless, odorless, tasteless liquid.

This unique combination capability, which characterizes all chemical compounds, is testimony of the highest order to that of a purposeful, intelligent master "Chemist" behind the scenes. Only a God of incredible power and knowledge could have orchestrated the millions of combinations of atoms needed to form the basic building-block substances of life.

As an example, take the deadly poison sodium and combine it with the deadly poison chlorine. The result is the naturally occurring substance NaC1, better known as salt. The next time you drink a cup of water, consider the source.

The Bee

They sting, make honey and provide us with one of the clearest proofs that there must be a God out there. So what is so special about a bee? Did you know that there are over 3,000 species that live in North America? One of these, the honeybee, is a fascinating communal creature, endowed with genius unmatched in both the insect and human realm.

If you ever look into a beehive, fascination would begin to build in your mind. The tiny honeybee has literally built an entire city of cells or cones. Each cell is always six-sided and all are in perfect symmetry. These cities can consist of up to 10,000 or 20,000 separate cells, and are produced from wax from their own bodies. The hexagonal shape was chosen by the bee because it knew that it would provide them with the maximum amount of storage space needed. The bee also knew that a six-sided construction would be must stronger than, say, a triangular or square makeup.

Bees, although they can't verbally communicate with one another, speak to one another through chemicals. Through this means, they can quickly give directions to others if there is danger nearby or to tell where the entrance to the hive is. Honeybees also perform a special dance for their coworkers when they have found the source of nectar. Amazingly, this dance indicates the direction as well as exactly how far away the honey is. Blessed with a keen sense of smell, the honeybee can tell if there is even one stranger bee in a hive of hundreds of others, by its odor alone.

One final quality of our friend the bee is that he is a marvelous thermostat. It is characteristic of the honeybee to keep the inside of their hives at a constant temperature of about 95 degrees Fahrenheit. Bees like it hot.

When the weather is cool bees cluster. They move around and breathe faster, thus raising their body temperature and heating up the hive. When it starts to get too hot, some bees act as air conditioners, fanning their wings, causing a breeze and cooling to come to the hive. Other bees bring water into the hive. They in turn are met at the entrance by coworkers, who take the water droplets and spread them around the hive. Still other workers go about the hive fanning their wings to evaporate the water and cool the hive. All of these actions bring the hive temperature back down to 95 degrees F. What wonderful teamwork, and just think—no costly heating or air-conditioning bills.

A bee can't read a book, can't speak a word, can't spell its name, nor does it even know it has a name. Yet the bees possess such creative and design powers that one has to wonder how such knowledge could have found its way into their tiny bee brains in the first place. But no one can deny that our little visit into his home, the beehive, has shown us behavior that has to be the product of a mind of great intelligence or a fabulous "God-given instinct."

A Positive Force

Our minds have been so conditioned in our society to rush, rush, rush, that we rarely seem to find time to stop and observe the wonderful creation all around us. The next time you are standing by a rolling brook, a river or a fountain, take time to stop and just allow the flowing or cascading water to permeate your consciousness. The therapeutic and calming value that flowing water has is truly remarkable.

From a majestic mountain range to a delicate red aromatic rose, mother nature has provided her children with a splendid showcase of rich and positive beauty. Why not sit back and enjoy the show? It's free to young and old alike.

Man by his very nature is in a perpetual state of motion; always striving to obtain things and advance himself. Calm and peaceful sailing are the exception rather than the rule throughout our lifetimes. Nature, on the other hand, has a way of generating peace, serenity and a gentleness all her own. The lessons she has learned, down through the centuries, she is always willing to share with those of us who have the time to stop and just observe.

Incredible complexity and profound simplicity are just two facets of our wondrous universe. We are left with but two options as to the origin of such majestic splendor. Either "in the beginning there was nothing. And by chance, nothing, by itself, became everything," or "in the beginning God created the heavens and the earth." I leave it up to the reader to ponder his options.

The first case represents one of despair. It presents us with little hope for finding meaning in our lives. The second offers us a great hope to find out what real living is all about, and what the ultimate purpose of life is. Before we explore this second option, let's see what proponents of the first one have to offer us.

The Dark Side Of The Moon

The occult, the New Age, humanism and Scientology are just a few of our modern answers to finding true meaning in life. What these "movements" have in common with the Bible is a fundamental belief that if we leave this planet without really finding out what life is all about, and why we are here to begin with, we must forever accept the following morbid scenario:

> If there is no existence to an answer whose question means our existence, then we are hopelessly trapped in a universe that has no meaning, no purpose and no way of escaping the inevitable conclusion that life is a concept that is as dead as our universe is dark. Our existence is thus one of only form and shadow reflecting out into a vast sea of eternal nothingness.

False Systems

In 1903 a young man named Nikolai Lenin with a small band of followers began his assault on the world. By 1918, his band had grown to over 40,000 and together they had gained control of a country of 160 million. Communist Russia was born and up until recently its former brand of government had taken control of one-fourth of the population of the world. With the coming down of the Berlin Wall, we hope, communism was given a partial death blow.

Communism on the surface has an appeal to it, but the reality of life to those under its influence is quite disheartening. It is basically a form of society where the means of production (e.g., land, factories, resources) are owned in common and all production is shared.

In communist countries today what has the average communist citizen gained? He has really gained very little except that he can consider himself to be part of a cause. On the negative side he has sadly been sold into bondage.

To those 1.5 billion souls who live under communist regimes, freedom has been stripped away. When you can't come and go as you please, when you can't speak whatever is on your mind and when the bookstores you visit are devoid of many of the books you might like to read, freedom becomes a dream and not a reality. We all know about the scarcity of material goods most communist countries live with. But on a far more serious note, when basic freedoms are taken away from us, we begin to lose our personhood and hope for real meaning in life.

Communism denies the existence of God, denies its society the freedom of speech and dictates to its citizens what life is suppose to be about. As these simple freedoms, which we in America so often take for granted, are taken away one by one, so too is the capacity for our freedom of thought.

With viewpoints on the issues slanted, with access to the Bible as well as certain other books of philosophy and wisdom forbidden in many countries and a belief in God intensely discouraged and belittled, what are we left with?

The result is a society of individuals whose thinking capabilities have been greatly impaired, by virtue of having vital access to our world's vast treasure chest of ideas withheld from them. In its place communist citizens are presented with a distorted view of the world around them.

They have been kept isolated in a chamber where total freedom of thought has only a small hope of ever entering or leaving. Imagine, the viewpoints presented in this book, whether good or bad or whether you agree with them or not, will most probably never be allowed to be shared with over one-fourth of the population of our world. Clearly light is needed to penetrate such darkness.

False Movements

Humanism is heralded by its followers as the ultimate answer to all of man's problems. Secular humanism, as it is often referred to, is a man-centered philosophy that places its confidence in the following five tenets:

- There is no God.
- Evolution is the process that brought man into existence.
- There are no such things as absolute morals.
- Man is the supreme crowning glory of the universe.
- Man is innately good.

As a result of this brand of thinking our society has seen itself going through one of the most dynamic transformations in its entire 200-plus-year history. With God vanishing from the picture, and no absolute standards acknowledged, America has traded in her Declaration of Independence freedoms for a new brand of counterfeit freedom.

In the last thirty years, the United States of America has become an increasingly humanistic society. Its proponents believe that we should be free to do anything we want to. They also believe that there are really no absolute rights or wrongs and that men by themselves can form a true utopian world. In return for following this ideology we have seen quantum leaps in the following:

- AIDS is now a runaway epidemic.
- Drug addiction is now spiraling out of control.
- Abortion is now genocide of incredible proportions.
- Homosexuality is now considered to be an alternate lifestyle.
- Child abuse is now a national horror.

When freedom in a society becomes unchecked, the inevitable result becomes bondage. Humanism is beginning to not only sweep across this great nation of ours, but to sweep it away also.

False Thinkers

If there is one thing our world has never been lacking in, it would have to be men of great thinking capacity. Names such as Darwin, Freud, Einstein, Marx, Plato, Aristotle and Lincoln can all be acknowledged as men whose viewpoints and ideas have had a great influence on our world. While many have had a positive impact on our lives, even long after they spoke and penned their wisdom, many have equally left a legacy of distortion and despair.

In the latter category the name of Sigmund Freud would have to be placed. Freud was the founder of psychoanalysis. This form of psychotherapy tries to treat people suffering from nervous disorders by asking the individual to recall painful experiences from the past that somehow are lodged in unconscious and subconscious thoughts. While this form of treatment is losing support today, the Freudian ethic, which

Freud popularized at the turn of this century, has shown little sign of releasing its hold on America.

What did Freud believe? Hal Lindsey summed up the Freudian view of man as follows:

> "The human race is motivated chiefly by pleasure; everything starts and ends with sex. Man is repressed by society in the fulfillment of his unconscious drive for gratification of his erotic desires; this repression makes him unhappy. The consequence of the conflict between our pleasure-seeking instincts and the repression exerted by our society is neurosis."

Lindsey further stated that "Freud firmly laid the groundwork for extreme permissiveness." (60)

Our sexually liberated society today can directly trace its roots back to Freud. The Bible views sex as a most beautiful experience that is reserved only for the marriage bed. If this boundary is ignored then sex no longer becomes a special union of two souls but a commodity bartered between two fleshes.

The result is an inevitable progression into the world of perversion and disease. Premarital and extramarital sex, homosexuality and lesbianism, incest, prostitution, sodomy, pornography, V.D., AIDS, sadomasochism, abortion and countless millions of destroyed families totally shatter the beauty that could have been.

Just what can we thank Freud for? Freud has become the father of a fractured fairy tale of fiction, where fast and free living have served only to foster a lifestyle of fatal attractions. Permissiveness has led to perversion. Peace of mind has been sacrificed in return for pleasure-seeking. Finally the stage has been set for danger in the years ahead.

False Freedoms

False systems, false movements and false thinkers all seem to offer the same thing to their followers, namely, false freedoms. As we have seen, communism talks equality but denies true freedom. Humanism offers us so much freedom that we turn it into a noose. Freud offers us freedom that perverts the soul.

Counterfeit freedoms are always a product of darkness. They masquerade as light but soon reveal their true nature as darkness. But there is still hope amidst all this darkness, for there still can be light at the end of the tunnel. True freedom is obtainable and our old friend the Bible has a few thoughts on how to find it, which we will explore in the final two chapters. We read in John 8:32, "…and you shall know the truth, and the truth shall make you free."

Light And Darkness

Nature, more appropriately called "the creation," is full of beauty, wonder and surprises. It is a very positive force, as we have seen throughout this chapter. Every facet of our natural world speaks of a purpose, and asks us to ponder just how such magnificence could have come into being. The Bible casts its vote in favor of divine design. It states that this great universe of ours is the product of a divine, omnipresent, omnipotent and omniscient Creator.

The forces of darkness, which we have discussed, have filled the ballot boxes with the names of a host of different candidates. Each of these candidates in the last analysis has brought with it despair, repression and depression. Darkness by its very nature can never lead us into the light.

It is only appropriate that the final stop on our journey should take us into a world of incredible possibilities, hope, beauty and meaning. A world where darkness is completely obliterated by a light of immense illumination that shines as brilliantly as the most glorious sunset in the twilight of a summer evening.

Chapter 9
Troubled Waters Or Calm Streams?

America today stands at the crossroads of her very existence. While she spends hundreds of billions annually on national defense, her number-one enemy is poised to launch a strike force of immense destruction. This enemy of impending disaster is herself. The stage is now set for self-annihilation as America braces herself to enter an era of Disintegration.

Era Of Disintegration

During the last forty years, the very fabric of this great country of our has been itself stretched, torn and mangled to the point where it is literally hanging together by a few threads. What we see today in our country is a severely fractured and dysfunctional society. In a land where such great prosperity exists, despair is spreading like a cancer, as unchecked epidemics run rampant throughout every sector of our population.

In our nation today the following is a partial listing of dysfunctional behaviors and lifestyles:

DYSFUNCTIONAL
BEHAVIOR/LIFESTYLE
Emotionally and mentally ill
Alcoholics
Homosexuals
Child abuse victims

Domestic violence (battered wives)
Abortions
Compulsive gamblers
Drug addicts
Divorces
Unwed mothers
Runaway children
Attempted suicides
Homeless
Incest victims

The real sad thing about this list is that it is incomplete and the sheer number of people falling into most of its classes continues to climb.

There is a great war going on in the U.S.A. today. These invaders are not from outside our nation, nor even from inside, as in the case of a civil war. But the war that is being waged lies within each individual. Our minds are being bombarded by thought bombs of megaton proportions. How much longer we can endure these attacks on our consciences, only time will tell.

Heating Up The Furnace

As we look at some of the causes for these breakdowns in the quality of life we see all around us, I believe that the seeds for solution will begin to become evident. How we plant and nurture them will hold the key to our very survival.

Television/Internet

The escapist comedy shows and adventure stories we once were accustomed to watching on our television sets now are mostly available to us only as reruns. Prime time is now reserved for a host of violent shows and sexually alluring sitcoms that would make grandmother shiver at their very sight.

Cable T.V. and especially the internet have brought adult entertainment into our living rooms. The videomania and DVD revolution that is going on has brought a veritable Pandora's box of mesmerizing chillers, killers and sexual thrillers into our personal libraries. As we continually play these visual themes over and over again, is it any wonder that these soap-opera sagas stamp their seducing messages permanently on our minds?

School-Based "Clinics"

In an effort to stop the epidemic rise of AIDS, V.D. and the hundreds of thousands of unplanned teen pregnancies each year, our government is now proclaiming our school-based clinics as the solution. As these so-called clinics become the law of the land, our schools will be able to dispense birth control to minors. This is like tossing gasoline on a raging fire. It's as if our government is throwing in the towel and hoisting up the white flag.

The only signals our children will receive by this decision is: If you are going to have sex, play it safe. Imagine a whole generation of youngsters growing up in an environment where safe sex is O.K. at any age. If our children are no longer required to have parental consent in one of the most important decision-making areas of their lives, will it be long before they start telling us, the parents, how we should run our lives?

When fundamental decisions regarding what's right and wrong for our children are involved, a parent, not some government agency, must have the final say. If our government continues to strip away sexual sanctions, we better brace ourselves for a new explosion of sexual permissiveness. Is it any wonder our youth are experiencing such a difficult time growing up, when our government is allowing adult decisions to be decided upon by mere babes?

Pornography

Child pornography is a national disgrace. Imagine: our children are being used in sexually explicit movies and real-life sexual perversions throughout our country. This trend is increasing at an alarming rate with no end in sight. Now this type of cancer has exploded on the internet and is almost uncontrollable.

A woman's breast, once considered an important organ of nourishment, is now revered as a god of total erotic pleasure. Sex, that once beautiful and most intimate of shared moments, reserved for the privacy of a husband and wife, is now little more than a commodity to be bought, sold, swapped and shared by anyone and everyone.

Sexual Suicide

With our T.V.'s, movies, internet, songs, telephone lines and magazines bombarding both young and old alike with sexual overtures, is it any wonder we have such trouble holding together and even starting families? Sexual freedom and perversion, coupled with meteoric rises in sexually based diseases, are generating ripple effects throughout our country.

AIDS is clearly a by-product of our sexually liberated society. AIDS is so devastating because it breaks down all of our disease- and germ-fighting mechanisms, causing our bodies to become powerless to defend ourselves from their invasion. I believe that AIDS may just be at the vanguard of a new wave of killer diseases too horrifying to even think about.

Despair Everywhere

The sexual dilemma we are experiencing today is just one area where despair is gaining a stronger and stronger foothold in America. As one examines the earlier list, the only logical conclusion is that despair is widespread in almost every area and walk of life. For the millions who exist in dysfunctional environments, mere survival has become their American dream. But what about the rest of our population? Most of these individuals are struggling just to make ends meet and stretch their paychecks to the next payday.

Fifty years ago, it was common to see families with four, five, or six children. Today a family with three or four children is considered a big family. To support a clan of five or six little ones today is almost financially impossible, especially if only one parent works. Yet we hear that the quality of life is far better now than when our grandparents grew up; is it really?

Many people in the work force start their careers with high hopes and enthusiasm, but this is often short lived. Disillusionment soon begins to take hold as job dissatisfaction becomes the rule rather than the exception for so many. Retirement planning often starts early, as hopeful employees contemplate the day when they won't have to work at jobs they never really enjoyed to start with.

Sadly, when they do reach this special time of life, age creeps up, and declining health often never allows them to truly enjoy these golden years they dreamed about for so long. Despair is everywhere and this is going on in the richest nation on the face of the earth.

Mixed Messages

Our airways are sending such inconsistent and hypocritical signals to everyone that our minds are being scrambled into shambles. Just what is right and what is wrong is becoming more difficult for us to discern. Consider as an example an old cigarette ad.

Newport had a cigarette advertisement that represented the ultimate in hypocrisy. The words "Alive With Pleasure!" were prominently displayed around men and women with smiles all aglow. The same ad, however, had a small rectangular box in the corner that read as follows:

SURGEON GENERAL'S WARNING: Smoking Causes Lung Cancer, Heart Disease, Emphysema, And May complicate Pregnancy.

Talk about mixed messages.

These words clearly tell all of America that our government is allowing a known carcinogen (cancer-causing agent) to be sold to a population who once they start using cigarettes, by and large, get hooked on and addicted to them. Our FDA (Food and Drug Administration) takes extraordinary steps to insure that any new drug brought to market is thoroughly tested for any adverse side-effects, both short and long term. Any known carcinogen would have an incredibly difficult time ever making it to the pharmacist's shelves. Yet Uncle Sam is sentencing millions of its citizens to a slow death as they puff their lives up in smoke.

With all of the new, tough laws being enacted, it is common to see supermarkets and discount stores prominently displaying "No Smoking" signs right above or below the large stockpile of cigarette cartons they have in stock. As a result of these mixed messages, the youth of our nation are growing up confused and bewildered.

Is There Any Hope?

The gloomy picture we have just painted somehow has fallen far short of the great American Dream scenario we all thought our birthright. How can a country with such great prosperity be in such a dismal state of affairs? Several years ago I began to ask myself this very question. In hopes of finding an answer to this great state of despair, the question of why we are here in the first place, if it is only to experience such a short-lived, mediocre existence, kept pounding away at my brain. Such thoughts began to flood my mind:

Have you ever wondered why you are here in this moment of time and space? Or perhaps one clear night, as you gaze into a brilliant, star-filled evening sky, your mind begins to ponder just how you came into existence. But most of all, in a quiet moment, when we are all alone, the question "Where are we going in this world?" inevitably becomes a resounding gong on the corridors of our minds. Yes, "why," "how" and "where" are the words that we begin to focus upon whenever we stop for a moment and turn our thoughts toward the realm of the infinite.

As I sit here and allow my thoughts to wander, I cannot help but feel an utter insignificance to life without knowing why I am here. Man, that crowning glory of all our world, since he first began to formulate ideas and concepts, and experience feelings, has asked the question "Why?"

Why am I here? Throughout man's existence, through each heartbeat, breath and step he has taken, the question of why has never ceased to leave his mind. Without the answer to this most fundamental question, life will never have meaning, man will never find true happiness and our journey through time will be one filled with despair, bleakness and a feeling of emptiness. Just examine your heart, for no secrets can ever be hidden from it.

Just when I thought I would never find the answer to all of my who, what, where and why questions and the reason for the despair I saw all around me, the answer came. Both the cause and the cure became abundantly clear to me, as I allowed the Bible to become part of my life.

The Bible: The Great Solution-Finder

With so many different books on the market claiming to be the answer to all of life's problems, how can we know which, if any, have merit? Movements, cults and different philosophies abound today.

Fortunately many Americans are skeptical and, before they are willing to listen to what these "problem solvers" have to say, require some sort of tangible evidence to their claims and positive credentials to their character. Before I present the Bible to you as the book that claims to show the cause for all of our problems and give their solution, I ask you to put the Holy Scriptures through the same two standards mentioned above: The tangible evidence and credentials test.

Worthy Of Respect

The Bible also asks one more question before you make your decision to either examine it or pass it by: Has the Bible earned your respect? The entire focus of my book, to this point, has been to present the Bible to you in a way that would peak your curiosity, appeal to your intellect, provide you with fascination, dispel the age-old myths surrounding it, and, foremost, earn your respect.

If it hasn't earned your respect, I ask you to stop right here and not finish this book. Perhaps that's the problem we face in our country today. We try so many different people's brand of thinking and philosophy without first gaining respect for them. Disappointment and disillusionment inevitably follow and so we move from one hope to another.

The Bible is a heavy book, and not only in physical weight. Its claims are indeed deeply profound. If the preceding eight chapters have helped the Holy Scriptures earn some level of respectability in your sight, then you owe it to yourself to read on, and at least consider the magnificent alternative this one great book of hope has to offer.

Tangible Evidence

The influence of the Bible in our society today is truly incredible. As we have seen, our government was founded on many of the principles of the Bible. Our great Ivy League schools for centuries used this one book as their ultimate textbook. Many of our greatest presidents, scientists and businessmen of the past put their trust in this one amazing volume of wisdom.

Our holidays are in many cases biblical in nature. "In God We Trust" is still boldly displayed on all of our coins. Year in and year out, the Bible is one of the best-selling books around. Concepts of morality are an integral part of America, because of this one book.

Our knowledge of history, science and mankind have been greatly enhanced by the influence of a 2,000-year-old book. Great literature, music and art have this one book to thank for their inspiration and composition.

The tangible evidence is indeed there that the Bible is a world book for all people and for all time. Whether you have read it or not, and whether you believe it or not, its influence and respectability are unmatched.

The Gideons

The Gideons International, a nonprofit organization, has insured that no matter where we travel in America or, for that matter, in the free world, the Bible is sure to be found. The Gideons are in the Bible-placing business. In every major hotel and motel room in our country, as well as in over 180 other countries worldwide, they have placed a Bible, free of charge, for any traveler to view while away from home.

Hospitals in many cases also have been supplied by the Gideons with this great book of spiritual healing. Even our jails, where permissible, have an abundance of Bibles on hand for the men and women who many times have no one to turn to but God as they try to piece together their broken and shattered lives.

In Fact, the Gideons place over 60 million Scriptures yearly in 180-plus countries and in over 80 languages, all at no cost to those they benefit. (61) No matter where we go in this land of ours or almost the entire world, it's hard to deny the Bible's influence or its physical presence.

Credentials

You may now be saying to yourself, "Why should I read the Bible as opposed to some other great book of inspiration or religion, like the Moslem Koran or the great books of Eastern thought? Or why not adhere to the wisdom of our great ancient philosophers like Aristotle or Socrates?"

Just what makes the Bible so different? As we have seen throughout this book, the Bible has met every challenge brought against it and defended itself most admirably. In every area of thought it has demonstrated itself to be a timeless masterpiece of wisdom and advice.

It is not only a book of history, it has made history. No book is more intellectually sound. It has been perfectly preserved for 2,000 years.

Finally, from every facet and angle we look at it, the Bible stands tall, head and shoulders above every other book ever written.

John MacArthur, Jr., in contrasting the Bible with other great sacred books and ancient philosophers, put it this way:

> "Take, for example, the sacred writings of the Hindus. They contain such fantastic nonsense as this: 'The moon is 50,000 leagues higher than the sun and shines by its own light. Night is caused by the sun setting behind a huge mountain several thousand feet high located in the center of the earth. This world is flat and triangular and is composed of seven stages; one of honey, another of sugar, a third of butter, and still another of wine. And the whole mass is borne on the heads of countless elephants which, in shaking, produce earthquakes.' That's ridiculous.

> "Read the Koran and you find that the stars are nothing but torches in the lower heavens, and that men are made out of baked clay. These gross errors abound in many writings. Errors regarding the material world are common in Homer, in Greek and Roman mythology, in the disordered books of the Hindus, and in the traditions of the Buddhists and the Moslems. The greatest geniuses of ancient philosophy, such as Aristotle, Plato, Pliny, Plutarch, Lucretius and others, wrote such absurdities that if one such absurdity were found in the Bible it would totally and forever discredit its inspiration. But there is not one such absurdity in the Bible." (62)

Has the Bible earned your respect? Can you honestly dismiss its profound influence in this great nation of ours and, for that matter, in the world we live in? Can one truly call himself a well-read individual without having read this one special book? Has the Bible begun to take on a new light for you as we have journeyed into its amazing pages? Finally, can it be denied that America is in danger of internal collapse? If you are in agreement with the above statements, then let the Bible present you with one final challenge: Examine its message.

Chapter 10
The Magnificent Alternative

The Bible has a magnificent alternative way of living to offer anyone with a desire to establish a personal relationship with its Author. May the following five biblical messages serve as your introduction to the God of the Bible and as your passport to eternity.

Message Number One – God Created Everything

Right from its very first words, the Bible puts us on notice that "in the beginning God Created the heavens and the earth" (Genesis 1:1). We read further (in Hebrews 11:3):

> *By faith we understand that the worlds were prepared by the word of God, so that what is seen was not made out of things which are visible.*

Evolutionists quickly run into problems in trying to explain origins. They contend that we evolved from simpler life forms, which over great expanses of time became more and more complex until humanity came about. They can offer us no clues, however, as to where the original inanimate matter came from.

Scientific theories such as the Big Bang bring us a little closer to the ultimate beginning of the universe. They, at least, postulate that somehow there was some sort of matter in existence, before it became everything. But, on logical grounds alone, the Bible goes the final step by acknowledging "that what is seen (our universe) was not made out of things which are visible."

In other words, there was nothing there to start with except God. But to have made a universe of such incredible size, amazing complexity, perfect orderliness, fabulous mysteries, and awesome beauty would have required a force of indescribable creative genius, possessing unlimited power and intellect that no finite mind (such as we possess) could ever completely fathom. The above description basically defines the God of the Bible, who created the stars, planets, mountains, trees, animals and, yes, you and me. Message number one states: You are clearly here because God created you—not by chance, but by deliberate design.

The Psalmist beautifully described this process and offered praise and thanksgiving to God:

> *For thou didst form my inward parts; thou didst weave me in my mother's womb. I will give thanks to Thee, for I am fearfully and wonderfully made; wonderful are Thy works, and my soul knows it very well. My frame was not hidden from Thee, when I was made in secret, and skillfully wrought in the depths of the earth. Thine eyes have seen my unformed substance; and in Thy book they were all written, the days that were ordained for me, when as yet there was not one of them.*
> Psalm 139:13-16

Message Number Two –
We Are all Born With A Sin Nature

Way back in chapter two we began to explain the biblical concept of sin. We saw how the first human beings on earth, Adam and Eve, lived in perfect harmony and fellowship with God. However, when they disobeyed God's command to not eat the fruit from the tree of the knowledge of good and evil, they committed sin.

The Bible goes on to tell us that everyone born since then has inherited this original sin nature. Romans 3:23 tells us, "For all have sinned and fall short of the glory of God." The Book of Jeremiah puts it this way: "The heart is more deceitful than all else and is desperately sick; who can understand it?" (Jeremiah 17:9)

It is our nature, the Bible tells us, to sin. And no matter how hard we try we, by ourselves, can never break out of its evil clutches.

Just what is sin? Simply put, it is any action or thought that we do or entertain that goes against what God, through His Word, the Bible, has told us is right and proper. It is this inborn sin nature that lies behind all of the problems we face in life. The great problems and despair we have seen throughout the last chapter can trace their origin back to our own evil natures.

The reason the alarming trends toward self-annihilation are increasing today is that our society, by and large, refuses to acknowledge this biblical view of ourselves. Instead, the official religion of our land has become one of secular humanism. As we saw earlier, one of its five fundamental tenets is that man is innately good.

To many people, sin is only something that other people do. To many, murder, stealing and adultery are all that sin encompasses. The Bible, however, says sin is much broader. The following two portions of Scripture will tell us what God views as sin:

> *And just as they did not see fit to acknowledge God any longer, God gave them over to a depraved mind, to do those things which are not proper, being filled with all unrighteousness, wickedness, greed, malice; full of envy, murder, strife, deceit, malice; they are gossips, slanderers, haters of God, insolent, arrogant, boastful, inventors of evil, disobedient to parents, without understanding, untrustworthy, unloving, unmerciful.*
> Romans 1:28-31

> *Now the deeds of the flesh are evident, which are: immorality, impurity, sensuality, idolatry, sorcery, enmities, strife, jealousy, outbursts of anger, disputes, dissensions, factions, envying, drunkenness, carousing, and things like these.*
> Galatians 5:19-21

Under this definition, we begin to see that sin is an integral part of our makeup. The above sins are outwardly expressed; but what about our sins of omission? Each year a new name of horror hits our headlines. Ethiopia, Somalia, Sudan and Mali represent millions of people who have literally starved to death through severe droughts and political escapades. Yet our silos are bursting at the seams with food and grain galore.

How can we sit back and allow tiny children and old folks alike to cry aloud for a few morsels of food when we throw out more than enough to feed them all. The answer is not just apathy, but sin. Sin is the great divider that not only separates us from fellowship with God, but from quality relationships among ourselves.

The main focus in our lives, because of sin, is not on God, or even others, but on self. Sin always seems to find us out when we examine the motive behind our actions. I share the following personal testimony to demonstrate the all-encompassing nature of sin.

> Back in 1981, I used to do volunteer work at a community center for mentally disturbed individuals in New York City. Twice a week I would donate my time to help feed, socialize with and listen to the problems of these hurting people. Years later, when I began to analyze my motives behind doing such a worthwhile activity, the answer suddenly became obvious. Back then there existed a great void in my life, and a desire to find meaning. I thought that this work would help fill that void in my life. The real reason behind my outwardly good deed was not to help others, but to help me.

As our society continues to drift into the fantasy world of humanism, believing in our innate goodness and that we can somehow solve all of our problems, our hopes for solutions become dimmer and dimmer. Message number two states: Our natures by themselves are prone to evil; just examine the evidence and your hearts. Someone once said in referring to the Bible, "Sin will keep you from this Book or this Book will keep you from sin."

Message Number Three –
False Gods Are Not The Answer

Man by definition is a religious creature. Down through the centuries, mankind has always had objects of worship, to which it has bowed down. The Greeks had their mythological gods such as Zeus and Apollo. Many primitive societies worshiped the heavenly bodies—the sun, moon and stars. Other tribes elevated stones and trees to "god status."

Even in biblical times, pagan societies erected statues as worship objects. Names such as Baal, Chemosh, Dagon, Molech and Nisroch were the temple and house gods that received genuflect treatment. In India today there are literally millions of statuesque idols to which families pay homage. The Bible categorizes all of the above under the caption "false gods." We saw earlier (in Deuteronomy 4:19) that God expressly forbids worshiping the heavenly hosts. As far as all the rest go, God says that they are nothing more than "...the work of man's hands, wood and stone, which neither see nor hear nor eat nor smell" (Deuteronomy 4:28). They by their very nature are useless when it comes to providing meaning and direction to our lives.

We immediately see the foolishness of this type of worship in our sophisticated, intellectual environment. We wonder how people can be so gullible. In our own quest for meaning, we have erected a whole new set of gods. One set of gods attempts to put us in touch with ourselves and place us on a higher plane of existence. These are what I like to call "system gods." A few examples follow.

TM

TM (Transcendental Meditation) is a system whereby we are taught to empty our minds and begin to mediate on a specific word called a mantra. But if we empty our minds, then how in the world can we ever find out who we really are? And how can we find out what life is all about if we have no facility left to think, analyze and ponder with?

EST

Another system, called est, was very popular in the 1970's and early 1980's. Est attempts to put people in touch with something called "experience." Through an intensive several-day seminar, participants are taught to just experience their experiences? Its founder, Werner Erhard, said, "Experience for us has no form to it; it's pure substance without any form." (63) Mind games would be a more appropriate name for this journey into never-never land.

The New Age Movement

Dust off secular humanism, add a few new twists, and lo and behold we now enter into the world of the "New Age Movement." This cosmic humanism, popularized by actress Shirley MacLaine, is becoming the new rage in American philosophical circles. New Agers believe:

- We are all gods.
- There is no death.
- Reincarnation is the mode of transportation from one life to the next.
- Humanity, the physical world and God are all deeply interrelated and flow together as one.
- Reality is only what we perceive it to be.
- We can transform our own consciousness and thus become masters of our own universe.
- All religions are one.

The New Age resembles a Chinese menu. We choose one philosophy of life from column "A," two concepts of God from column "B," and one view of humanity from column "C." Its appeal is quite popular as evidenced by the fact that our major bookstores have a whole section reserved for books on the movement.

The New Age is basically a compilation of the best of man's past ideas on how to find meaning in life. These ideas have been modernized somewhat and repackaged for today's space-age society.

As with any movement, its followers claim that it is the ultimate answer to all of our problems in life. Of course it, therefore, must tell all of mankind before our present age that they were wrong in their belief system. If asked where its concepts of God, life and death, reality, higher consciousness, and religion come from, the New Age proponents would have to answer: man's mind.

What the New Age Movement in the final analysis is telling us is as follows: While each one of the pieces in its overall philosophy of life was unable, by itself, to give man the meaning he so desperately has been searching for, the sum of all its parts is.

The New Age Movement, in every one of its tenets, is diametrically opposite to what the Bible teaches. If this movement is right, we must then throw out all of our Bibles. Before you do this, however, don't forget to put the "New Age" under the tangible evidence and credentials test; see if it is "worthy of your respect."

Atheism

Even the atheist worships a god called self. With no god to believe in he places himself as the supreme person in his universe, and spends the rest of his life searching for a reason for his existence. Searching every pathway, every byway, overturning every stone, examining every philosophy, and experiencing every feeling, as he comes to the end of his journey, the answer he finds is that none exists.

The Bible says that false "system gods" can never solve our problems or satisfy our hunger for meaning. Colossians 2:8 admonishes us:

> *See to it that no one takes you captive through philosophy and empty deception, according to the tradition of men, according to the elementary principles of the world, rather than according to Christ.*

Substance And Substitute Gods

The other type of false gods we worship in America today allure us with their charm and their prospects for a rewarding future, then place us under their yoke of bondage. These "substance" and "substitute" gods are deceptive deities and come in a curious array of sizes and shapes.

To over 10 million citizens of our land, god is found in a bottle. The alcoholic has a special relationship with his bottle that few people are allowed to violate. It's his preoccupation, passion and permanent companion, to which he swears complete allegiance. Under her influence, all hope for a rewarding life is literally smashed "on the rocks." Proverbs 20:1 warns, "Wine is a mocker, strong drink a brawler, and whoever is intoxicated by it is not wise."

Another type of false hope comes on four legs and has fur all over its body. Horse racing is a billion-dollar business. So many people are hooked on these horses that they call the track their second home. Poker chips, dice and slot machines have cast their mesmerizing spells on millions. For this growing percentage of our population, the only thing that is a sure bet is that they always seem to remain behind the "eight ball."

Heroin, cocaine and crack offer instant highs to anyone willing to trade his soul for a one-way ticket into the land of the living dead. Millions of Americans have allowed these mind-altering chemicals to permanently place a trip back to reality, a dream that can never come true. For those individuals, bowing down to these goddesses of pills and powder is no longer an option but an obsession.

The Holy Scriptures clearly warn us that these false "systems," "substances" and "substitutes" can only lead us into slavery. They offer hope, but never seem to deliver. They masquerade, the Bible says, as "angels of light," but soon reveal themselves to be producers of darkness.

Message number three states: False gods can never lead one to the truth; just ask their worshipers. Proverbs 14:12 says, "There is a way which seems right to a man, but its end is the way of death." The Bible not only continually alerts us to this fact, but exposes the father figure behind it all, as message number four graphically depicts.

Message Number Four – Satan Is Our Real Enemy

What do the following names have in common: Beelzebub, the great red dragon, Lucifer, the old serpent, the tempter, the devil, the wicked one, the god of this world, the angel of the bottomless pit, the father of lies, the prince of the power of the air, the enemy? They all represent different names the Bible uses to refer to Satan. (64)

Being born with a sin nature helps us to understand why it is so difficult to cope with the day-to-day struggles we encounter. But what went on behind the scenes, leading up to our inheriting this nature, is essential to our understanding the need for God's magnificent alternative, soon to be unveiled, in our final message, number five.

The devil, in the form of the serpent, right from the very beginning of humanity, inhabited the same garden of Eden as did Adam and Eve.

He wasted no time in enticing Eve to break the command of God regarding the tree of the knowledge of good and evil. Genesis 3:1 tells us,

> *Now the serpent was more crafty than any beast of the field which the LORD God had made. And he said to the woman, "Indeed, has God said, 'You shall not eat from any tree of the garden'?"*

The serpent went on to tell Eve,

> *You surely shall not die? For God knows that in the day you eat from it your eyes will be opened, and you will be like God, knowing good and evil.*
> Genesis 3:4-5

The rest is biblical history. Eve took a bite, gave some to Adam to eat, and sin entered the world. A logical question you might be thinking is: Where did the serpent come from?

The Scriptures tell us that the serpent was not always a "beast of the field," but a creature of incredible beauty, wisdom and power. Before God created the earth there existed a vast army of created spirit beings called angels. These angels spend their entire eternal lives in worship and praise to their Creator.

One of them, named Lucifer, was the ultimate in perfection. He was created by God, perfect in every way. Indeed he was the ultimate angel. The Bible tells us that angels are higher than man in many ways, such as power and wisdom. They, however, have one thing in common with you and me. Angel or man, we are all given a free will by our Creator, to make our own decisions.

Adam and Eve made one fatal mistake in the garden. They exercised their free will in disobedience to God. As a result, fellowship with God was broken, sin entered the world, and death came through sin.

The writings of the prophet Ezekiel begin to tell us a little of the background behind the magnificence of this most supreme of created spirits, Lucifer. For we read:

You had the seal of perfection, full of wisdom and perfect in beauty. You were in Eden, the garden of God; every precious stone was your covering: The ruby, the topaz, and the diamond; the beryl the onyx, and the jasper; the lapis lazuli, the turquoise, and the emerald; and the gold, the workmanship of your settings and sockets, was in you. On the day that you were created they were prepared. You were the anointed cherub who covers, and I placed you there. You were on the holy mountain of God; you walked in the midst of the stones of fire. You were blameless in your ways from the day you were created, until unrighteousness was found in you.
Ezekiel 28:12-15

Another prophet, Isaiah, informed us of the nature of this unrighteousness:

How art thou fallen from heaven, O Lucifer, son of the morning. How art thou cut down to the ground, which didst weaken the nations. For thou has said in thine heart, I will ascend into heaven, I will exalt my throne above the stars of God: I will sit also upon the mount of the congregation, in the sides of the north: I will ascend above the heights of the clouds; I will be like the Most High.
Isaiah 14:12-14 KJV

Ezekiel 28:16 completes the picture:

By the abundance of your trade you were internally filled with violence, and you sinned; therefore I have cast you as profane from the mountain of God...

Lucifer exercised his free will and became so puffed up with pride that he wanted to be God. A great rebellion in heaven followed, and Lucifer, along with one-third of the angels, was cast out of heaven and sentenced to eternal banishment. (See Revelation 12.)

While Lucifer's sentence is permanent, God has allowed him to roam the earth until the final day when this world of our comes to an end. As Satan, he still possesses his great power and has used it to plague mankind from day one.

He indeed is the father of lies, the great tempter and the reason behind all the wickedness and perversion that exists today. Ephesians 6:12 says,

> *For our struggle is not against flesh and blood, but against the rulers, against the powers, against the world forces of this darkness, against the spiritual forces of wickedness in the heavenly places.*

These names all refer to the demonic influences that inhabit our planet.

If this long account of how evil entered our universe seems fantastic to you, I would agree with your assessment. If any other book but the Bible were to present such an incredible fantasy-like account, I would have my doubts also. But the Bible, as we have seen, is like no other book ever written.

The evil deeds of man, as well as the author behind them, Satan, are an integral part of all sixty-six books of the Bible. The Bible devotes an inordinate amount of time to the influence this one fallen angel and his horde of demonic companions have had on mankind.

The fact that this definition of how evil came into our world is expounded upon by a book of such amazing respectability should at least cause one to ponder its plausibility. This, coupled with the fact that the evidence of evil we see today worldwide fits remarkably well with the sin-and-Satan account, adds further weight to its believability.

Could it just be possible that the quantum leap in perversion we see occurring during the past twenty-five years is correlated with the equally explosive rise in the number of books on the occult? Bookstores today now devote entire sections to the occult arts. Witchcraft, sorcery, astrology, spell casting, omen interpretation, satan worship, and a host of other satanic practices can be found in almost any bookstore. We are strictly admonished that "…whoever does these things is detestable to the LORD…" (Deuteronomy 18:12)

There are evil forces all around us that are supernatural in nature and clearly not the product of "flesh and blood." These invisible motivators of evil are taking captive more and more people every day. How else can we explain the following phenomena:

> Over 10 million Americans are hopelessly addicted to alcohol and drugs. They, if need be, will lie, cheat, steal and even kill to obtain these substances that deep in their hearts they know are poisoning their bodies and destroying their minds.

Or what could possess millions of parents to beat their small, helpless and precious children to the point where scars become permanent, tears never stop flowing and smiles are miles apart? Child abuse is evil personified. And what about those millions of husbands who, perhaps only years earlier, vowed to love and cherish their wives "till death do us part," and now beat them routinely as if their wives were punching bags? Or what type of irresistible force causes one American every minute to attempt suicide?

These are extreme cases, you say. Then how about the cases where we allow situations that never materialize in our lives to place a hole in our stomachs. Worrying is the number-one pastime in our country and ulcers her close associate. Or the tens of millions who willingly allow poisonous cigarette smoke to patrol their airways and lungs.

There is something sinister and invisible all around us that is robbing us of the peace of mind, joy and quality of life for which we so yearn. No matter how hard we try, thoughts of lust, bitterness, envy and jealousy, which we hate so much, never seem to want to listen to our commands when we tell them to leave. Message number four states: We have an invisible enemy who has taken control of our lives. Satan is his name.

But thanks be to God, for redemption is available to the entire world in a most spectacular way. The ultimate answer to every question you have ever asked is now ready to be revealed in our final message.

Message Number Five –
Jesus Is "The Way, And The Truth, And The Life" (65)

Back in chapter two we introduced Jesus Christ as the central character of the New Testament. We are now ready to explore His claims, which are as fantastic as His influence is vast. Jesus claimed to be, among other things, the Son of God, the savior of the world, and the author of eternal life. I hope that the pages of this book have prepared you for the following divine encounter. We are now ready to allow the infinite glory of God to become a part of our very being.

A Question

Before we examine the great and precious promises that God says are available to all of us, let me answer one final question that may be on your mind. Someone once asked me: If God knew that we were all going to sin in the first place, then why did He allow us to, and why did He give us that capacity?

The answer to this honest question puts us in touch with the very essence of the nature of God. First John 4:8 tells us in three words that "God is love."

It is the very nature of God that He can do nothing but love. When He created the angels and mankind, it was always His desire to have fellowship with them. Sharing His great love and blessings with His creation is what God enjoys most. While He wants obedience from us, His love will not allow it to be something He would ever compel us to do. God could have made us robots and thereby obtained complete obedience, but it wouldn't have been loving obedience.

Godly love in its purest form gives freely to others without ever demanding reciprocation. So God took a chance with us and gave us all free will to either accept Him or reject Him. We have unfortunately chosen the latter and broken our fellowship with our Creator.

Perfect Plan

God knew that Lucifer would sin, and that he in turn would cause Adam and Eve and then us to follow suit. Yet His love for us constrained Him to implement a plan so ingenious and so incredibly loving that no playwright has ever been able to match this script in terms of intense drama, joy and triumph.

Let us now look at why Jesus came to earth, and the magnificent salvation plan of which He was the focal point. In light of what we have learned about ourselves from the first four biblical messages, let me summarize this plan. After this, I will expand on its meaning for us today and the host of incredible promises God has reserved for us.

As infinitely loving as God is, He is also perfectly holy. If you were to find a small black spot on an otherwise nicely pressed suit or dress, I dare say you probably would not want to wear it outside. Back to the cleaners it would go. Imagine now that you were going to have a personal meeting with an infinitely holy God. Bringing your whole lifetime of sins into His presence surely would not start off this meeting well.

In fact, Romans 6:23 says, "For the wages of sin is death…" When we sinned, we not only broke fellowship with God, but we permanently and eternally separated ourselves from His presence, as well as from any hope of having a personal relationship with Him. God can never tolerate even the slightest sin entering His holy presence or kingdom.

As a result all mankind, by virtue of our sinful nature, is spiritually dead, with our souls sentenced to spend eternity in the same place to which Lucifer (Satan) was banished. A literal Hell was originally "…prepared for the devil and his angels" (Matthew 25:41), but our sins unfortunately will destine us to this same place of eternal fire and agony.

Thus the dilemma: A God of great holiness and mankind of great sinfulness, and a chasm between the two that is infinitely wide. Our eternal Father could not bear to see His creation endure such a tortured existence. His love made it necessary to leave us the option to either obey or disobey Him. But His love also had a provision, to restore us to fellowship with Him, even if we chose to sin. His holiness demanded payment for sin, and His love offered pardon.

Enter Jesus

The great God of all eternity decided that, in order to reconcile these two opposite conditions, He would send His son, Jesus Christ, to earth, to satisfy both. Born to a virgin (Mary), who was impregnated by His very Holy Spirit, Jesus came into this world almost 2,000 years ago. The genius of the person of Jesus Christ is that, as a result of this human/divine union, He was born both fully human and fully God. Impossible, you might say, incredible—yes, certainly; but this is exactly who the pages of Scripture tell us Jesus was.

Being fully human, Jesus was able to experience all the emotions, pressures and trials you and I live with. Until the time of His death at age thirty-three, He was tempted in all areas of life, yet, unlike us, He never sinned. God's plan was to send Himself, in the form of a human being (Jesus), to earth to demonstrate a perfectly sinless life and then sacrifice Himself as our sin-bearer. Jesus would take our sins and their penalty onto Himself.

When He was crucified on the cross at Calvary, He literally took the entire sin load of all humanity—past, present and future—onto His body. Leading a perfect, sinless life, gave Him the right to sacrifice Himself on our behalf, for our sins. Second Corinthians 5:21 says,

> *He made Him who knew no sin to be sin on our behalf,*
> *that we might become the righteousness of God in Him.*

Since He was also God, He could consider our great debt to Himself as now paid in full. Jesus was the great sacrifice, the cross the place where our sins were nailed, and His resurrection from death three days later our assurance that our pardon was complete.

Our part in this wonderful plan is to accept God's free gift of salvation and the complete pardon from all our sins. God asks us:

- to acknowledge that we are sinners.
- to repent of our sins.
- to ask Jesus Christ into our hearts.
- to believe that He is the Son of God.

The moment we make this decision and turn our lives over to Jesus, something totally amazing happens: We become transformed creatures. Second Corinthians 5:17 says, "Therefore if any man is in Christ, he is a new creature; the old things passed away; behold, new things have come." In addition, we are promised eternal life in the process.

We are not only pardoned from our sins, but God has fused His very own divine nature into our souls. By the grace of God, we now become

His precious little children. We read (in Romans 8:16), "The Spirit Himself bears witness with our spirit that we are children of God."

With our fellowship with our Eternal Father restored, and our future reservations in Hell cancelled, we are now ready to experience a whole new dimension of life. As Christians we now possess a new capacity not to sin. Yet, since we are still in our human fleshly bodies, we still may sin. But this time there is a big difference when we do sin.

Remember, we saw that Jesus died for all our sins: past, present and future. When we do sin, we know that the penalty has already been paid for by Jesus. First John 1:9 beautifully tells us what to do if we sin in the future: "If we confess our sins, He is faithful and righteous to forgive us our sins and to cleanse us from all unrighteousness." The key word is "confess!"

A Dilemma

As a thinking man ponders the reality of Jesus, he must inevitably come to one of two conclusions: That He was who He says He was or that He wasn't; or, for that matter, that maybe He never really existed.

If Jesus was the Son of God and His story is true, then I dare say reading the Bible is something everyone would want to do. The offer and chance to have eternal life is a pretty strong motivation, in my mind. However, the teachings of Jesus also present us with an equally strong motivation of a different variety. To not believe in Jesus and repent of our sins causes us to bear the penalty for those sins ourselves. This penalty is eternal separation from God and the banishment of our souls to a literal Hell. Indeed, if Jesus was real, the bookshelves in our bookstores should not have too many Bibles left on them.

What if Jesus existed but His claims were not true, either distorted or presented as outright lies? And for that matter, maybe He never really existed, but was a mythological character, a made-up tale such as the Greek god Zeus.

The implications of this statement are most startling and alarming. If the most influential person in the history of humanity and the most impact-making book are a lie or at best a hoax, then our entire world and its history have been molded by a lie and not the truth.

This goes contrary to our very nature, where the quest for the truth and reality are part of our fundamental being. How could a lie set the tone and the pace for so much of what we are today. This one concept should in and of itself provide a most provocative motivation to read the Bible. Proverbs 12:19 (TLB) provides a most interesting challenge to your intellectual mind. It says, "Truth stands the test of time; lies are soon exposed."

The Bible has withstood the test of time. But for it to have withstood this test and be based on a lie or a hoax would without question make the most fascinating reading ever conceived, just to ponder and find out how this could be.

So, unlike most dilemmas, which lead us to choose between two different alternatives, there really is no dilemma with the Bible, but only one alternative: It demands to be read, because its claims are so amazing, whether you believe them or not. In addition, its influential nature is so far-reaching.

Abraham Lincoln summed it up best when he said,

> "I decided a long time ago that it was less difficult to believe that the Bible was what it claimed to be than to disbelieve it." (66)

This book is too hot to let it lie dormant and unopened as it does in millions of homes throughout our country. In these homes the only time it is touched is to remove the dust that has accumulated on it through neglect.

For those of us who believe that Jesus is God I pray that the following few thoughts will serve to strengthen your faith and deepen the joy that serving Jesus can bring. For those of you who are still skeptical I hope that these closing observations will begin to excite you and introduce you to a whole new dimension of living that you have been searching for all your life.

New Life

As a new child of God, we receive the most precious gift imaginable. The very Holy Spirit of God now comes to make His abode in our bodies. The Bible refers to this Spirit as our teacher, guide, comforter and eternal companion. The Holy Spirit is always there to help us along the way in our walk in life.

God still requires us to obey Him in all the things His wonderful Word, the Bible, says. However, as we start to read and study the Bible, it now begins to become alive and totally illuminated to us through the spiritual enlightenment of the Holy Spirit. As a result, obedience to God now seems to make so much sense.

Picture for a moment the parent/child relationship. As a loving father or mother, we realize that our precious little children (especially from the ages of birth to three) almost exclusively depend upon us for every facet of their lives. They place their total trust in our hands. While we should always allow our children to voice their opinions and express their feelings, we must equally make it clear to them that we require complete obedience to us. We must have the final say on all matters.

So many times they will pout, cry and throw tamper tantrums, demanding to get their way. We in our knowledge and experience must deny these requests because, unlike our children, who have so little understanding, we know that it would be bad for them if we gave in to their demands. And when they do disobey us, many times a harsh word or a whack on the behind must be administered to them—not to hurt them, but because we love them.

Discipline hurts us as we see them cry; but the intent is always for their benefit. We require obedience and administer punishment to help our children grow up properly. Our superior wisdom, our knowledge of the harmful effects of bad decisions, and our insights into the future, coupled with our disciplinary love, are some of the best gifts we can ever give to our children.

This is exactly the same relationship our heavenly Father wants to share and have with us. God is all-knowing and He knows what is always best for us. The only way He can shower us with all the wonderful promises and blessings His Word says are now ours is to require us to obey Him. We saw earlier how John D. Rockefeller's health declined and improved in direct proportion to his obedience to God's eternal laws.

As we follow the precepts of the Bible we can rest assured that our lives will be full of abundant blessings. But if we choose to disobey God and His wonderful teachings from the Bible, we have only ourselves to blame if our lives don't turn out the way we wished they could have. God has a wonderful plan for each of His children, for we read:

> *For I know the plans that I have for you, declares the LORD, "plans for welfare and not for calamity to give you a future and a hope."*
> Jeremiah 29:11

During the last fifty years in America, we have increasingly gone astray from the biblical teachings our country was founded on. The dysfunctional, decaying society we see today is the result of this disobedience.

Since I have come to trust Jesus Christ as the Lord, Master and Savior of my life, I can speak from firsthand experience that His promises are magnificent and His blessings real. May I now whet your appetite a little with a few of God's choicest promises from His incomparable Word, the Bible.

The Trade-In

The annual pastime for millions of Americans is to trade in their old (and not so old) used cars toward the purchase of a brand-new car. Unfortunately this annual event is never ending. When you invite Jesus Christ into your life, the transaction becomes a permanent, one-time trade-in. We saw earlier in (Second Corinthians 5:17) that "...the old things passed away; behold, new things have come." Just what are these old and new things?

The old things consist of our old nature. In this exchange we get to trade in our problems with envy, worry, jealousy, prejudice and lying. We get to unload the alarming stress we place our bodies under. The booze, gambling, drugs and host of other addictions so many of us have can also be thrown in free of charge.

In return we have traded up for our new creation models, equipped with a host of options.

Fully reclining peace, automatic joy and an eternal warranty on all of our parts are just a few options that are standard equipment for all of God's children. What a trade-in: To get rid of the things we never wanted in the first place and to receive in return the things we really want out of life.

Meaning

Just who are you? Where are you going in life? And why are you here in the first place? Without a firm knowledge of a definite God, the only answers to these three questions can be: I am nothing but an insignificant speck in a universe of infinite dimensions. My destination in my short life of seventy to eighty years is back to eternal nothingness. And the reason I am here is because my great-great-great-etc. grandparents, who were nothing but random molecules, one day, by chance, happened to collide.

When we become a member of the family of God, through Jesus the Son, meaning of incredible magnitude becomes our permanent possession. These three who, where and why questions now finally make sense.

God's Word tells us a little about who you now are:

> *The Spirit Himself bears witness with our spirit that we are children of God, and if children, heirs also, heirs of God and fellow-heirs with Christ...*
> Romans 8:16-17

Imagine being a joint-heir with the Creator of the universe. That's exactly who the Bible says we are.

Our final resting place is no longer the grave as you may have thought before, but the eternal watering hole of God: Heaven. First John 5:11 (KJV) is quite clear on this point:

> *And this is the record, that God hath given to us eternal life, and this life is in His Son.*

Finally, the reason we exist is just plain exciting to see. First, we now live to give glory to God. Just as a little child receives the greatest satisfaction possible by doing things that please his parents and make them proud of him or her, we now live to please our heavenly Father. This we do through worshiping Him and praising His holy name.

Second, we exist to help other people in all areas possible. Ephesians 2:10 says,

> *For we are His workmanship, created in Christ Jesus for good works, which God prepared beforehand, that we should walk in them.*

Finally, we were created to be the recipients of a great myriad of blessings, both present and future. Great peace, unspeakable joy and a real purpose for living are now ours: gifts from our wonderful Father. And we already know that everlasting life is our future reward.

Negatives As Positives

Being a Christian does not exempt us from going through trials and temptations, as well as the necessary disciplinary actions our heavenly Father must administer from time to time. Certainly no one likes trials and discipline, but in each case there is a divine purpose behind them. James 1:2-4 puts it beautifully when it says,

> *Consider it all joy, my brethren, when you encounter various trials, knowing that the testing of your faith produces endurance. And let endurance have its perfect result, that you may be perfect and complete, lacking in nothing.*

Trials are for our benefit. They help build us up so we can give more glory to God. Trials also help us help others going through similar situations, since we have been there before. Finally, difficult situations help strengthen our faith in God, as we see how He wonderfully brings us through them.

When we do something wrong as children, we soon come to realize that some sort of disciplinary action is going to come our way from our parents. It is no different in the case of how our heavenly father is going to treat us when we step out of line.

> *Furthermore, we had earthly fathers to discipline us, and we respected them; shall we not much rather be subject to*

> *the Father of spirits, and live? For they disciplined us for*
> *a short time as seemed best to them, but He disciplines us*
> *for our good, that we may share His holiness.*
> Hebrews 12:9-10

God's discipline is to help bring us back into close fellowship with Himself, so He can continue to share His vast storehouse of blessings and holiness with us. Only our great God can turn every negative situation into a positive experience.

The Ultimate Promises

In the final book of the Bible, Revelation, we are treated to a sneak preview of what heaven will be like when we arrive there after our physical journey on earth ends. The first thing we notice is that no matter how much pain, suffering and sickness we may have had to experience here on earth, they will all forever vanish in heaven. Revelation 21:4 declares:

> *...and He shall wipe away every tear from their eyes; and*
> *there shall no longer be any death; there shall no longer*
> *be any mourning, or crying, or pain; the first things have*
> *passed away.*

As we continue in our Christian walk, we begin to see victory after victory become more and more a part of our lives. The more time we spend in prayer, Bible reading and communion with God, the lighter our burdens become. In the past, before we knew Jesus, problems always seemed to get us down and get the better of us. Now, armed with knowledge of God's Word and with prayer, we overtake our problems and become overcomers. As overcomers in Christ, the Book of Revelation describes what we can expect to see:

> *... To him who overcomes, I will grant to eat of the tree of*
> *life, which is in the Paradise of God.*
> Revelation 2:7

*He who overcomes shall thus be clothed in white garments;
and I will not erase his name from the book of life, and
I will confess his name before My Father; and before His
angels.*

Revelation 3:5

*He who overcomes, I will make him a pillar in the temple
of My God, and he will not go out from it any more; and
I will write upon him the name of My God, and the name
of the city of My God, the new Jerusalem, which comes
down out of heaven from My God, and My new name.*

Revelation 3:12

*He who overcomes, I will grant to him to sit down with
Me on My throne, as I also overcame and sat down with
My Father on His throne.*

Revelation 3:21

*He that overcometh shall inherit all things; and I will be
his God, and he shall be my son.*

Revelation 21:7 KJV

Wow!

Think About It

Well, we have come to the end of our journey. My sincere hope is that this book has challenged you to think about perhaps adding the Bible to your list of books to be read in the near future. As this great nation of our continues to drift into deeper and deeper troubled waters, the Bible might just be the life preserver that can stop us from sinking.

If your life is not really what you want it to be, the Bible has an alternative way of living that could be the answer you are looking for. If I were ever in a position to give this one magnificent book a subtitle, I think it would read: "The Most Intellectually Compelling Book Ever Written." Why not pick up a copy today and watch it revolutionize your life.

Source Notes

Chapter 2

1. James Strong, *Strong's Exhaustive Concordance of the Bible* (Nashville, Tennessee: Thomas Nelson Inc., 1979), Publisher's Preface.

2. John MacArthur, Jr., *Is the Bible Reliable?* (Panorama City, California: Word of Grace Communications, 1982), pp. 75-76.

3. "The Holy Bible—Wholly True" by Winkie Pratney. Copyright 1979, 1984. Last Days Ministries.

4. *The New Encyclopaedia Britannica*, Macropaedia, 15th Edition (Chicago: Encyclopaedia Britannica, Inc., 1986), Volume XXII.

5. John MacArthur, Jr., *Is The Bible Reliable?* (Panorama City, California: Word of Grace Communications, 1982), p. 98.

6. Josh McDowell, *More than a Carpenter* (Wheaton, Illinois: Tyndale House Publishers, Inc., 1988), p. 8.

Chapter 3

7. *The Rebirth of America* (Philadelphia: Arthur S. DeMoss Foundation, 1986), p. 13. (Words by Katharine Lee Bates).

8. Ibid., p. 15.

9. *The Rebirth of America* (Philadelphia: Arthur S. DeMoss Foundation, 1986), p. 31.

10. Ibid., p. 37.

11. Ibid., p. 37.

12. Ibid., p. 37.

13. Laurence J. Peter, *Peter's Quotations-Ideas for Our Time* (New York: Bantam Books, Inc., 1989), p. 43.

14. *The Rebirth of America* (Philadelphia : Arthur S. DeMoss Foundation, 1986), p. 37.

15. Ibid., p. 37.

16. Ibid., p. 41.

17. "The Star Spangled Banner," by Francis Scott Key, *The World Almanac & Book of Facts* (New York: Newspaper Enterprise Association, Inc.,1978), p. 477.

18. James Robison, *Save America to Save the World* (Wheaton, Illinois: Tyndale House Publishers, Inc., 1980) p. 105.

Chapter 4
19. S.I. McMillen, *None of These Diseases* (Old Tappan, New Jersey: Jove Publications, Inc., 1981), p. 11.

20. Ibid., p. 11.

21. Information provided by The Institute for Creation Research, Santee, California.

22. 93 Supreme Court 705 (1973), Justice Blackmun.

Chapter 5

23. Memorable Dates, *The World Almanac and Book of Facts* (New York: Newspaper Enterprise Association, Inc., 1978), p. 713.

24. Henry H. Morris, " Creation and the Seven-Day Week,"*Impact Series,* Institute for Creation Research, San Diego, September, 1979, p. 1.

25. Definition of "Eternity," *The American Heritage Dictionary of the English Language* (New York: Dell Publishing Co. Inc., 1978), p. 247.

26. Ibid., Definition of "Infinite," p. 365.

Chapter 6

27. Werner Keller, *The Bible as History* (New York: Bantam Books, Inc., 1980), Introduction, p. xxv.

28. Howard F. Vos, *Beginnings in Bible Archaeology* (Chicago: Moody Press, 1978), p. 9.

29. Ibid., p. 66.

30.Werner Keller, *The Bible as History* (New York: Bantam Books, Inc., 1980), p. 10.

31. Howard F. Vos, *Beginnings in Bible Archaeology* (Chicago: Moody Press, 1978*),* p. 89.

32. Werner Keller, *The Bible as History* (New York: Bantam Books, Inc., 1980), p. 267.

33. *The New Encyclopaedia Britannica,* Micropaedia, 15th Edition (Chicago:Encyclopaedia Britannica, Inc., 1986), Volume I, p. 36.

34. Werner Keller, *The Bible as History* (New York: Bantam Books, Inc., 1980), p.50.

35. Ibid., pp. 49-50.

36. Henry M. Morris, *Men of Science: Men of God* (El Cajon, California: Master Books, 1988), pp. 99-101. (Chart partially adopted and modified).

37. "Creation or Evolution? Part II-The Historical Record" by Winkie Pratney. Copyright 1980, 1983. Last Days Ministries.

38. Henry M. Morris, *Men of Science: Men of God* (El Cajon, California: Master Books, 1988), pp. 23,26.

39. Ibid., p. 85.

40. *Dictionary of American Maxims*, compiled by David Kin, (New York: Philosophical Library, Inc., 1955), p. 40.

41. Ibid., p. 40.

42. Ibid., p. 40.

43. Ibid., p. 40.

44. Ibid., p. 40.

45. *Webster's New World Dictionary of Quotable Definitions*, edited by Eugene E. Brussell, (New York: Webster's New World, 1988), p. 48.

46. *Dictionary of American Maxims*, compiled by David Kin, (New York: Philosophical Library, Inc., 1955), p. 40.

47. Henry M. Morris, *Men of Science: Men of God* (El Cajon, California: Master Books, 1988), p. 47.

48. Josh McDowell, *More than a Carpenter* (Wheaton, Illinois: Tyndale House Publishers, Inc., 1988), pp. 47-48.

49. F. F. Bruce, *The New Testament Documents: Are They Reliable?* (Grand Rapids, Michigan: William B. Eerdmans, Publishing Co., 1980), pp. 16-17.

50. Howard F. Vos, *Beginnings in Bible Archaeology* (Chicago: Moody Press, 1978), pp. 47-48.

51. F. F. Bruce, *The New Testament Documents: Are They Reliable?* (Grand Rapids, Michigan: William B. Eerdmans, Publishing Co., 1980), p. 20.

52. Werner Keller, *The Bible as History* (New York: Bantam Books, Inc., 1980), p. 425.

53. *The New Encyclopaedia Britannica,* Micropaedia, 15th Edition (Chicago:Encyclopaedia Britannica, Inc., 1986), Volume III, p. 937.

54. "The Holy Bible-Wholly True" by Winkie Pratney. Copyright 1979,1984. Last Days Ministries.

Chapter 7
55. Col. Frank Borman, "Message to Earth," *The Guideposts Treasury of Faith* (New York: Bantam Books, Inc., 1980), p. 405.

56. Kenneth N. Taylor, *Creation and Evolution* (Wheaton, Illinois: Tyndale House Publishers, Inc., 1977), pp. 29-31.

57. Russell V. DeLong, *So You Don't Believe in God?* (Grand Rapids, Michigan: Baker Book House, 1977), p. 70.

58. Ibid., p. 71.

Chapter 8
59. Hal Lindsey, *The Terminal Generation* (New York: Bantam Books, Inc., 1980), p. 81.

60. Hal Lindsey, *Satan Is Alive and Well on Planet Earth* (New York: Bantam Books, Inc., 1984), p. 79

Chapter 9

61. Statistics provided by The Gideons International, Nashville, Tennessee.

62. John MacArthur, Jr., *Is The Bible Reliable?* (Panorama City, California: Word of Grace Communications, 1982), p. 73.

Chapter 10

63. Hal Lindsey, *The Terminal Generation* (New York: Bantam Books, Inc., 1980), p. 80.

64. Beelzebub - Matthew 12:24.
    Great red dragon - Revelation 12:3.
    Lucifer - Isaiah 14:12 (KJV).
    The old serpent - Revelation 12:9 (KJV).
    The tempter - Matthew 4:3.
    Devil - Matthew 4:1.
    The wicked one - Matthew 13:19 (KJV).
    The god of this world - II Corinthians 4:4.
    Angel of the bottomless pit - Revelation 9:11 (KJV).
    Father of lies - John 8:44.
    The prince of the power of the air - Ephesians 2:2.
    The enemy - Matthew 13:39.

65. John 14:6.

66. Hal Lindsey, *The Terminal Generation* (New York: Bantam Books, Inc., 1980), p. 106.